Bandroom Jottings

by PAUL HARVEY

EGON PUBLISHERS LTD.
Royston Road, Baldock, Hertfordshire SG7 6NW, England

Published in 1989
by Egon Publishers Ltd.
Royston Road, Baldock, Hertfordshire SG7 6NW, England

Copyright © Paul Harvey

ISBN 0 905858 47 6

Designed and printed
by Streetsprinters
Royston Road, Baldock, Hertfordshire SG7 6NW, England

All rights reserved. No part of this book may be reproduced or transmitted in any form or by any means, electronic or mechanical, including photocopying, recording or by any information storage or retrieval system without permission in writing from the publisher.

Contents

Frontispiece	iv
Acknowledgements	iv
Foreword	v
Introduction	vii
Mainly Autobiographical	1
Travel	13
Hippos and Humour	35
Verse	56
Uncle Paul's Problems	65
The Saxophone	83
Reviews	94
Kneller Hall	117
World Saxophone Congress	127
Woodwind Workshop	138
The London Saxophone Quartet	148
Publications for Clarinet	162
Publications for Saxophone	164

The author jotting in a typical bandroom

Acknowledgements

To WALLY HORWOOD, who did most of the real work in putting this book together. My own function was mainly that of a virtuoso with scissors and Sellotape, so my thanks are also due to the various magazines whose back numbers I assaulted in this fashion: Woodwind World, International Clarinet, Saxophone Symposium, Clarinet and Saxophone, Crescendo, Fanfare, Music Teacher, Winds, etc. . . .

The two principal photographers whose work appears in this book are GERALD STYLE and MICHAEL FARNHAM.

Foreword BY JACK BRYMER

In retrospect, I find that possibly the greatest surprise which awaited me upon my entry into the profession of music-making, at the somewhat geriatric age of 32, was the discovery of a corporate sense of humour. Having quitted, without regret, the rigours of the school-room, I was not without a deep appreciation of the subtleties of 4th-Form humour — and to find it still alive and in rude health, practised by the super-intelligent artists who were my new associates, was a revelation and a delight.

That there has always been an urgent necessity for such a safety-valve can be in no doubt. A musical ensemble is unique among human aggregations in one respect. Day after day, week-in, week-out, they are sharing a common experience. You don't pop out for a coffee to find out what old Jones has been up to for the past couple of hours, you know. What is more, the delights and frustrations are all shared, all absorbed, and all commented upon, albeit in terse and appropriate language, when opportunity arises. These comments are mostly concerned with the common enemies — conductor, 'fixer' ('contractor', then, if you so prefer) and the many purveyors of dread 'squeaky-gate' compositions. It is a love-hate relationship with them all, because in almost every case these worthies are also old 'pros', and speak the same language. The exceptions are terrible to behold, long to suffer, and quite soon forgotten when they depart. Conductors, in particular. Every orchestra is looking for a conductor to love, and life, if such a being is found, is indeed sweet. There are some who fit into this category, and many who do not. The former become everyday delights, the latter simply evil legends who live on in almost folk-lore tales much longer than they deserve — but always with a sense of chuckle rather than shudder.

It must be remembered that in every musical combination there are many who are there for what seems to be a quite unsurpassing reason. They love music. If they did not, you may be sure they would be employing their extremely high IQs in outwitting stock-markets or undertaking sinister financial manoeuvres which might well make them rich, if they could in fact retain their freedom. As it is, there is no hope. Midas was no musician (unless you count the odd second-fiddler who somehow convinces everyone he is the world's greatest conductor, and becomes a millionaire overnight). So these bright beings plod on, observing, noting and just occasionally commenting upon the strange world they occupy.

It is when they write that just a few of them display a surprising lucidity and style which sets them apart from the rest. Many of these have a 'throw-away' technique which is not always apparent, at any rate upon first contact. I recall one or two serious-seeming articles about bassoon-playing in a very highly technical magazine published in the USA, written by one of our very greatest performers upon that weird bag of tricks. These were taken quite seriously by many earnest students of the day. They were in fact 'spoofs', one and all, and a careful reading of the 'fingerings' revealed a rather embarrassing *double-entendre* which few have appreciated to this day.

It is this casual use of the 'in-joke' which makes musicians' humour quite deep and at times many-layered. I first noted this in Paul's writing some years ago in just such a similar magazine, this time British. Many readers took his report of a remarkable trio quite literally. They were, it seems, a clarinettist, a conductor/director, and a famous pianist, and after quite a while it emerged that their names were Sheik, Rattle and Roll. If you get this, that's fine. If not, you just haven't the equipment to appreciate the sort of humour I'm talking about, or perhaps your musical horizon isn't wide enough. It doesn't matter, because what follows is a lot of fun, and will be enjoyed by all sorts of people, knowledgeable or just plain ignorant. I hope you fit into one of these categories.

Jack Brymer

Introduction

Why Bandroom Jottings?
Because the life of a professional musician is rather like that of a soldier on active service; long periods of waiting interspersed with sudden bursts of hectic activity.
A well-known musicians' catch-phrase is 'Hurry up and wait'! Having written quite a lot of music ever since my student days, I suddenly discovered, about twenty years ago, that writing words is much easier than writing music. Rarely, however, have I been able to indulge in the luxury of sitting at home at my desk, at least for the initial writing of an article, though, of course I have to sit there to type out the fair copy.
All my life I've had this crippling handicap of having to go out and earn a living, mostly by blowing into variously shaped tubes. (Strange why people should pay you to do that, really, isn't it? I often wonder what a Martian visitor would make of it). So most of my writing is scribbled in odd bursts in bandrooms, while waiting to go on for concerts, or at rehearsals, in tacet sections, or on recording sessions during balance tests and playbacks. Indeed, I am writing this foreword in a school, where I have a free period, owing to a pupil having chickenpox!
In my everyday teaching I've always been a firm believer that if you can amuse somebody with a point, they'll always remember it by association with the joke. I know this for a personal certainty from my own language learning activities. (I can order beer and enquire where the toilet is in more languages than any other contrabass clarinet player in East Twickenham)! For instance, that favourite Spanish snack, the 'soap sandwich', which always reminds one that 'soap' is 'jabon' but 'ham' is 'jamon'.
I think that music, in general, labours under an intolerable burden of insufferable pomposity which imbues much of the writing on the subject with that quality of implied elitism which puts most ordinary people off it completely. In my writing I consider it my duty to make my small contribution to the universal dissemination of musical ideas by deflating as much of this pomposity as possible. This paragraph itself, is, of course, extremely pompous; I intended it

to be so. I make no excuse for underlining the obvious in pointing that out. If I'm setting out to deflate musical pomposity, then I must start with myself. If you set yourself up to be a music critic and write about other people's playing and composition, then you must be opinionated and exude an air of omniscience. It's only a leavening of humour which makes this acceptable in human terms. If George Bernard Shaw had reviewed any concert or composition of mine, I wouldn't care how abusive he was as long as it was funny. In fact, an unfavourable but funny review from a writer like GBS would be of more benefit to one than a run of the mill favourable one as readers would remember your name by association with humour. Who was it who said, 'It doesn't matter what people say about you, as long as they say something?' Either Confucius or Zsa Zsa Gabor, I think.

So, I hope that my two decades of jottings may provide you with a few points of interest about the clarinet and saxophone, hopefully interspersed with the odd chuckle here and there.

Paul Harvey,
Twickenham 1988

With my daughter, Paulina.

1 Mainly Autobiographical

EARLY DAYS IN SHEFFIELD

I was born in 1935, at Nether Edge Hospital, and lived for the first seventeen years of my life at Bents Green, Ecclesall. My first school was Ecclesall Church of England School, Ringinglow Road, until, at the age of eleven, I won a scholarship to King Edward VIIth School. That is where my musical memories start, in the form of singing in the school choir and being taken to Halle Schools Concerts at the City Hall. It must have been about then that I saw Benny Goodman in a film at Greystones Picture Palace and became fascinated by the clarinet.

I began hanging around Milner's Music Shop, which was then on Pinstone Street, every Saturday morning. The manager was an ex-professional musician called Norris Gregory, who really started me in my career, as he showed me how to play my first note on an old simple-system clarinet and introduced me to the finest clarinet teacher in the North of England, who lived in Crookes, and was to be my teacher for the next five years: the late Bill Tomlinson. Bill was the clarinet and alto saxophone player at the Empire Theatre, and was well-known all over Yorkshire for his clarinet recitals and schools concerts.

He was a superb teacher, both of technique and interpretation, and to this day I feel guilty if I allow one of my students to get beyond the first page of a Brahms' Sonata in the first half hour of a lesson. I can imagine Bill, looking down from the Great Bandroom in the Sky, saying, 'Aye . . . t'lad always were a bit slap'appy wi' 'is Brahms!'

Unfortunately he had a mental block about the saxophone, which he considered a necessary commercial evil, on no account to be studied seriously. When I was fourteen, he decided I was going to make a professional player. He enrolled me in the Musicians' Union and took me down to the Empire where the Pantomime was in its third month. In a corner of the bandroom was a vintage alto sax in a case charred by an incendiary bomb during the Blitz.

'There y'are, lad,' said Bill, 'there's t'saxophone; 'eres t'fingering chart and t'Panto parts; you're doing t'matinee tomorrow,' and he beat a hasty retreat to the nearest pub while I frantically prepared myself for my professional debut.

Over the next three years I deputised for Bill regularly, and was engaged in my own right to play second to him when the orchestra was augmented. The sight reading experience was invaluable, as the staple fare in those days was Twice-Nightly, Quick-Fire Variety, with occasional weeks of such shows as *Glamorous Nights on Ice*, or *Naughty Nudes of 1949*. I used to go to the Theatre straight from school and do my homework in a corner of the bandroom.

My first solo playing was done at King Edward's in various enterprising school concerts organized by Mr N. J. Barnes, the music master. These always included a clarinet duet by myself and Peter Fisher, who is now an English teacher at Cambridge.

My other most frequent concert appearances at that time were the monthly Chamber Concerts at the Victoria Hall, promoted by the late John Parr, a well-known professional bassoonist, ardent musicologist and lovable eccentric. He was a small, plump old man, with a round pink face and straggly white moustache, his bulging waistcoat usually rich in egg-stains or crumbs, and his feet invariably shod in heavy hobnail boots, with enormous tags sticking out behind.

He lived in a big house near Crookes Junction, full of antique instruments and piles of music. If I went straight to his rehearsal from school he would invite me into his kitchen for a pint mug of strong tea and a hunk of bread and condensed milk. He lived in the kitchen when not engaged in musical activities, and in one corner was his bed, containing his bassoon, wrapped in the blankets to keep the wood from cracking in cold weather. Often the kitchen would be full of bicycles festooned with strings of onions, sleeping bags and several bereted Breton onion-sellers. Apparently he often wandered about the continent in search of rare music and instruments, and when in Brittany would stay at the onion men's farms, returning their hospitality when they came to ply their wares in Sheffield.

Another rather quaint job was the Annual Police Parade. We used to assemble at the Central Police Station, and were driven to a Sports Field in a 'Black Maria'. I never discovered where it was as we were shut in! On arrival the motley collection of members of the Empire and Lyceum Orchestra and various dance bands were issued with ill-fitting ceremonial Police uniforms and proceeded to march up and down the field masquerading as 'Sheffield Police Band'. The fee, I remember, was ten shillings and as much beer as you could drink!

This was also the era of the great Traditional Jazz revival and I used to play in a group called 'The Red River Jazz Band', doing mostly Youth Club jam sessions. We were never serious rivals to the big time 'Smoky City Stompers' and I suspect that we enjoyed ourselves very much more than our audiences!

Concurrent with all this, I was gaining knowledge of the symphonic repertoire with the Sheffield Philharmonic Orchestra, under Herman Lindars. Also in 1949 (the year of the *Naughty Nudes*, you remember) I became a member of the National Youth Orchestra of Great Britain and three years later won a scholarship to the Royal College of Music.

My five years as Sheffield's answer to Benny Goodman were over but Bill Tomlinson's fine teaching and the varied musical experience I had gained in my lively home town were to stand me in good stead throughout the rest of my career.

THE SOLDIER'S TALE
(Paul Harvey — Not Stravinsky)

Sometimes, as the setting sun sinks slowly behind the Kneller Hall bandstand, my pupils — exhausted by their eight hours of unrelenting scales, long notes, dims'n'doms, arpeggios and finger-twisters — seek a little innocent relaxation by asking their aged Professor to tell them a story.

'Tell us about when *you* were in the Army,' they clamour, sitting cross-legged in the twilight; youthful faces glowing with eager anticipation.

Actually, *my* military service took place during the early 1950s, but as most of my pupils are under 20, this era seems as remote to them as the Napoleonic wars, in which they retrospectively participate at the end of each Grand Concert during the summer.

Like all Guards bands at that time, the Irish contained about 20% of young students from the Royal College of Music, doing their three years of National Service.

The Band was very high-powered musically, having gained a fantastic reputation during the war when it contained some of the top London orchestral players, and the Director of Music, Captain

C. H. Jaeger, hereinafter referred to as 'Jiggs', was determined to keep this up.

It was taken for granted that one measured up to this musical standard — otherwise one would not have been there — but even more demanding was the high standard of humorous repartee expected from even the lowliest members, and gauging the narrow dividing line between this and military indiscretion.

On one of my first guard mountings I stood quivering on the square at Wellington as Jiggs progressed through the ranks, chatting amiably or otherwise with members of the band. Upon confronting me, he prodded my (then) skeletal chest with his baton and demanded, in tones of mock severity: 'Where are your medals, Harvey?'

Knowing by now what was expected, I did my best: 'Gone to be cleaned, sir.' Jiggs shook his head sadly, and moved on.

On the next guard, the question was repeated. I produced my improved answer: 'Their weight was pulling my tunic out of shape, sir.' So it went on, at every guard for weeks. 'Lent them to the Band Colour Sergeant, sir' ... 'On loan to the Imperial War Museum, sir' ... 'I haven't earned any yet, sir, but I shall continue to do my duty in the hope of eventual recognition.' The last elicited his habitual response — 'Steady, now!' Which meant he conceded that my repartee was gaining some degree of Mick polish.

On the next guard, I heard him asking a new recruit in the rank behind: 'Where are *your* medals, Bloggs?'

Parade ground repartee with any other officer was dangerous, of course. I shared a garret in Pimlico with Colin Bradbury, now principal clarinet of the BBC Symphony Orchestra. The rent was 30 shillings (£1.50) a week, our pay being £3.10s (£3.50). We lived on a staple diet of beans on toast, the tin being opened with a bayonet and the contents heated in a mess tin over an ancient gas ring.

One day, the Adjutant of the New Guard took it into his head to inspect the band's bayonets; an unheard-of affront!

After several sharp scuffles necessary to wrench out blades firmly rusted into scabbards since the end of the war, the Band Sergeant's notebook was filling up with names, and the Adjutant was definitely twitchy. On reaching Colin, he snatched out his bayonet and recoiled in horror at the reddish-brown blade.

'Good God, man ... what's this on your bayonet? Blood?' 'No sir,' replied Colin, 'It's bean juice, sir!' Unfortunately, the Adjutant did not consider gastronomy a fitting hobby for a Guards musician.

The Band Colour Sergeant at that time was the legendary six feet, eight inches tall bass drummer, Nobby Clarke. Many contemporaries will remember his sonorous delivery of the order which starts the massed bands' part of Trooping the Colour: 'Twoooop!' ... followed by his bass drum solo: THUDDDD ...

Impressive as this was, I always considered Nobby's finest hour to have been at that point on our first tour of America when it became known that the promoter had gone broke, and it would be necessary for the band to work its passage, by a succession of Army camp concerts, back into Canada and across to Montreal where the return flight was booked.

I think it was in Detroit where we assembled around Nobby as usual to receive our next orders. 'Right, lads,' boomed Nobby, completely dead-pan. 'Orders ... ten o'clock ... Tuesday ... Montreal ... *Make your own way!*'

Connoisseurs of drill movements in general, and Trooping the Colour in particular, will be familiar with the Spinwheel. This is a complex manoeuvre performed only on this occasion by the Massed Bands of the Brigade of Guards, its purpose being to enable a band of five times the normal width to wheel in a comparatively confined space.

The effect in the middle of the enormous band is very strange; one minute you are marching along, playing away, orderly ranks of bearskins stretching in all directions.

Suddenly, up at the front, five Drum Majors' maces go up, and all hell breaks loose. Everyone starts going in different directions; the shape of the band seems all wrong. You hear countermelodies in the march that you've never heard before, because some of the trombones are pointing *at* you.

I remember this part of my first Trooping very well. I even recall the atmosphere in the middle of the band; a smell of damp bearskins, Bluebell brass polish and Household Cavalry droppings — the scrunch of hundreds of boots on the gravel of Horse Guards Parade.

Suddenly, I had an uneasy feeling that all was not as it should be. The men around me had the wrong-coloured plumes in their bearskins, the wrong number of buttons on their tunics, the wrong insignia on their collars. In the melee of the Spinwheel I had wandered into another band! ... And blundered into a burly figure wearing three gold stripes and a sash. '----' orff back to the Irish, sonny!' it snarled.

Panic stricken, I looked wildly around and saw some green plumes bobbing in the distance. The only thing I could do was to make a bee-line for them and, thankfully slid back into my hole in the bosom of the Micks. Only just in time.

As the Spinwheel completed its erratic gyrations, and as orderly ranks and files gradually emerged from the chaos we set off across Horse Guards again. It was then that I became aware that the person next to me was not playing an instrument.

Swivelling my eyes to the right, I saw it was Jiggs. He swivelled his to the left — and we eyed each other under our bearskin fringes. 'Welcome home, Paul Harvey!' he said.

Of many humourous exchanges during band practice, my favourite recollection concerns the band pianist, who resented having to play the clarinet in full band and made a fetish of never wiping it out. 'Here, smell my mouthpiece,' was his usual greeting.

He always sat with his particular crony at the end of the third clarinets, to which portion of the front line Jiggs was fond of directing a sudden beady eye, singling out a suspected skiver and ordering: 'Play that bit on your own.' One day he dropped on this reluctant clarinettist, whose reply was: 'Sorry, sir, I can't.' 'Why not?' snapped Jiggs.

Indicating his adjacent crony, the musician replied: 'Because it's *his* turn for the reed today, sir.' 'Steady, now!' replied Jiggs, and left the third clarinets alone for weeks.

The whole thing is summed up by a remark I once heard passed by a morose Grenadier to a bored Coldstreamer, as all five bands were standing about at Wellington one pay day. 'How is it,' he grunted, 'that whenever you see the Irish they're always laughing at something?'

CLARINET PLAYING IN BRITAIN

I've always been an indefatigable reader of American woodwind magazines, and have noticed that whenever writers are attempting to classify various national schools of clarinet playing, they become bewildered by Britain. Some writers mention the few British players who are well known in the USA - Reginald Kell, Gervase de Peyer, Jack Brymer and, more recently, John Denman.

My first clarinet at the age of twelve.

One way to spend your 18th birthday. The young soldier at Caterham in 1953.

Niagra Falls, 1954.

Taken during my first tour of Canada and USA in 1953.

P.H. in full frontal bearskin.

Lieut-Colonel C. H. Jaeger as Director of Music, Irish Guards.

Paul Harvey, extreme right, third row, with the Irish Guards Band in 1954. In the centre is Captain C. H. Jaeger, Director of Music, and, fifth from left, front row, is Band Colour Sergeant Frank 'Nobby' Clarke. Other well known woodwind players whom you might not recognise, looking so young are: Colin Bradbury, 5th from right, second row; Colin Courtney, 5th from left, second row; Christopher Hyde-Smith (flute), extreme left, top row; Geoffrey Wareham (oboe), 4th from right, top row; Bill Hudson (flute) 2nd from left, second row.

But this only makes them more confused, as all these players sound quite different from one another. Other writers give up any attempt at classification and ignore Britain altogether, while still others say, rather irritably, 'There is no school of British clarinet playing.' In fact the last group is right, but it's nothing to get irritated about. There is certainly no shortage of fine clarinetists in Britain, but there is no British 'school' as such — just a lot of individuals doing their own thing, according to their musical tastes.

I've just passed the 30-year mark of my clarinet playing career, and feel in the mood to set down some of the changes and developments I've observed over these three decades. I took up the clarinet in 1947, in Sheffield, England, a large northern industrial town, at that time in a terrible state of devastation following the German bombing raids of the early 1940s. Music, however, was thriving; there were two theatres with professional orchestras, several amateur orchestras, innumerable choirs and bands, and the Halle Orchestra came over from Manchester once a week to give a symphony concert. I was lucky enough to have lessons with a really fine teacher named William Tomlinson, then in his 50s, who in his youth had studied with both Charles and Haydn Draper, leading members of a family which dominated English clarinet playing in the 20s and 30s and taught most of the older players with whom I came into contact in my younger days.

Billy Tomlinson would certainly have been in the ranks of leading clarinettists had he gone to London as a young man, or taken the job in the Halle Orchestra which had been offered to him in the past, but he was not personally ambitious, and preferred to stay in Sheffield playing at the Empire Theatre, painting landscapes, and philosophizing in the pub. As a player he was a link with the old Draper school, which might be defined as trying to sound like a German on French instruments. He played on a very old pair of rosewood Buffets, with a very straight, solid sound. In the 1920s he had taught Reginald Kell who came from York, to the north of Sheffield. Tomlinson seemed to accept the 'controversial' Kell vibrato, but wouldn't let me, or any other pupils, indulge in such an eccentric habit!

Although I had all the early Kell recordings, my first conception of clarinet sound was entirely formed by listening to the man who bestrode the British clarinet scene like a colossus at that time — Frederick Thurston. Most of my early knowledge of the symphonic repertoire was gained through listening to the radio, and as Thurston was principal clarinet of the BBC Symphony Orchestra it was he that I first heard playing most of the orchestral solos. In 1949 I did an audition for the National Youth Orchestra of Great Britain and was accepted. A wonderful opportunity, as Frederick Thurston was the woodwind coach. So there I was, working under my idol at the age of 14!

Thurston was the greatest exponent of the nearest thing there has been to a British school which centered more around a particular instrument than a style of playing. That is, of course, the large bore '1010' clarinet manufactured by Boosey & Hawkes. All through my early years as a clarinetist, the prevalent idea in Britain was that all top symphonic players used 1010s, except for a few non-conformists who preferred the smaller bore 926 Boosey & Hawkes model. But within the 1010 school there was a schism; even as Thurston graced the BBC Symphony Orchestra with his massive, straight sound, the Royal Philharmonic Orchestra appointed a new principal clarinetist, an ex-schoolteacher and Royal Air Force physical training instructor who had bypassed all the conventional stages of formal study at music college — but who needs all that if you're a great natural player like Jack Brymer! Brymer carried Kell's ideas a stage further, producing the most vibrato of any serious clarinetist up to that time. He was teaching at the Royal Academy of Music, and Thurston at the Royal College of Music, so two opposing schools were beginning to gather; both playing 1010s, but vibrato polarized at the Academy and straight at the College.

In 1952 I won a scholarship to the Royal College of Music, and girded my loins to enter the fray as one of Thurston's firm-jawed disciples. Alas, before the year was out, the great man was dead. I continued my studies, after returning from three years' National Service, with Ralph Clarke, who had been Thurston's second and had now taken over the principal position in the BBC Symphony. I had enormous respect for Ralph's playing and his detailed knowledge of the orchestral repertoire, which benefitted me greatly in the profession. Although he played very much in his style, he did not have the charisma of Thurston (indeed, nobody could have) to gather a school of disciples around him.

By the time I left the Royal College of Music, there were no longer definable schools of playing connected with the College or Academy. Owing to the increasing popularity of the clarinet both establishments appointed more professors, so that several different styles were intermingled at each; John Davies, a Thurston disciple, was now teaching at the Academy, and Sidney Fell, more of the Kell school, was teaching at the College.

My first symphony job was as bass clarinetist of the Scottish

National Orchestra, which led to my interest in the larger members of the clarinet family. On returning to London to freelance, I acquired the third Leblanc contrabass clarinet to come to England, and gradually added more of the Leblanc family — basset horn, alto, E flat, etc. — Leblancs being the only complete family readily available here at that time. This caused me to forsake the 1010 school, as I decided to give Leblanc B flat and A clarinets a try as well. As I was doing a lot of saxophone playing I had to practise vibrato for that and gradually came to use it more on clarinet. Old habits die hard and though I use vibrato nearly all the time on saxophone, I tend to play clarinet straight unless I make a conscious decision to use vibrato for a certain passage.

In the 1960s I was playing often with the BBC Symphony Orchestra and went back on to 1010s, as the two principal clarinetists were Colin Bradbury, a very straight Thurston disciple, and Jack Brymer. I often had to play second with either, which provided me with excellent experience at matching two very different 1010 sounds.

When I was appointed to my present position as Professor of Clarinet at the Royal Military School of Music, Kneller Hall, I decided I should have a spell on all the top makes of clarinet, so I could advise my pupils on their perennial question, which is best? from personal experience. I first acquired a pair of Selmers, and then Buffets, which I am still using. Perhaps the biggest change in clarinet playing here in the last ten years has been the opening of an extremely energetic UK branch of Buffet-Crampon, which has transformed the British clarinet scene from (very roughly) 80 percent 1010/20 percent others, to something like 40 percent Buffet/40 percent 1010/20 percent others.

There seems to be more fine players about than ever before; if any of the London orchestras come your way on their many tours look out for: John McCaw in the Philharmonia (for me, possibly the best sound to be heard in Britain today, tending to the Kell style, minimal vibrato, and as near perfect intonation as anyone could wish for); Jack Brymer now in the London Symphony Orchestra; Bob Hill in the London Philharmonic Orchestra; Colin Bradbury in the BBC Symphony; and Prudence Whittaker in the Royal Philharmonic Orchestra, a younger member of our fine school of lady clarinetists of whom Thea King (Frederick Thurston's widow) and Georgina Dobree are the best known members. There are many highly individual recitalists with distinctive and often controversial sounds and repertoire such as Alan Hacker, John Denman, and Anton Weinberg.

Most significant of all, there seems to be a sudden upsurge of really frightening teenage virtuosi. For instance, the young New Zealander Mark Walton, who has settled here, and the 16-year-old Michael Collins, who recently became nationally famous through a TV Young Musicians Competition and is brilliantly fulfilling a hectic schedule of solo appearances. The next 30 years look really interesting.

2 Travel

My travels have fallen into three categories: first, a twenty-year kaleidoscope of uncountable thousands of miles in orchestra buses, hundreds of forgotten hotels and concert halls ranging from the Concertgebouw, Carnegie Hall and the Gewandhaus to Bournemouth Winter Gardens. This era overlapped with the London Saxophone Quartet tours; more civilised to travel with three companions than ninety three, we always used to say. In its turn, the LSQ period gave way to eventual solitary wanderings as clinician, soloist and adjudicator.

The early orchestral tours do not feature much in this book, as I was not into journalism at that time. However, one episode remains in my mind as an illustration of international rapport between clarinettists, or some such inspiring message.

In the course of an orchestral tour involving Amsterdam to Warsaw by coach (not all at once, fortunately!) we stopped at a border post between East Germany and Poland (or maybe between Czechoslovakia and Hungary). Our passports were taken away into the guardhouse for checking, and we just sat there, waiting and waiting, tired, hungry and thirsty, wishing we could get on towards the next place, wherever that was.

Eventually, the interpreter got back on the bus, accompanied by a border guard straight out of a James Bond film. Blackened teeth with silver fillings snarled through unshaven jowels hanging over the red stars on the grey uniform collar; coarse black hairs bristled on the ham-sized fists grasping the automatic rifle across the barrel chest. This hero of the People's Republic of wherever it was glared round the bus with suspicious, red-rimmed eyes, and we all sunk lower in our seats, trying to look less like reactionary counter-revolutionary capitalist hyenas.

The interpreter broke the ominous silence:

'This gentleman wants to know,' she said, 'if there are any clarinet players on this bus.' As it happened, the clarinet section was sitting together. 'This is it, chaps,' I whispered to the other three, 'the end of the line. He's going to take us out and shoot us!'

Concealment was useless; our loyal colleagues were already pointing us out. The black and silver teeth rattled off a burst of Slavic invective, which sounded to me like:

'So, clarinettist dogs, we have ways of making you talk, before we take you out to face the people's democratic firing squad.!'

But the interpreter did not agree with my translation; she said, 'The gentleman says he is an amateur clarinet player, and reeds are very difficult to obtain here, unless you are in one of the State Orchestras. He wonders if you have a few old reeds you could spare him?'

We were relieved and grateful to root around in our cases and produce a boxful of assorted reeds between us. He accepted this tribute with much flashing of black and silver teeth and garlic-scented thanks. Then he dashed into the guardhouse, returned with all the orchestra's passports, opened the border barrier and stood waving happily as we sped off to our next bath, drink and meal.

I have often wondered if he kept himself entirely supplied with reeds in this fashion from the various symphony orchestras which cross and recross that part of Eastern Europe.

'GO WEST, MIDDLE-AGED MAN'

The American Single Reed Workshop, now in its 5th year at Towson State University, Baltimore, is the brainchild of Dr Joseph Briscuso, Professor of Saxophone at TSU and Edward Palanker, bass clarinettist of the Baltimore Symphony. There was so much for me to admire and learn in the four days that it's only possible to mention a few highlights.

On the first full day my personal strain at having to give my first clarinet clinic and solo recital in the USA was amply recompensed by the friendly reception of the audiences, and the benefit I derived from listening to the other clinicians, notably Ralph Morgan on acoustics and Eugene Rousseau on saxophone high tones. The evening recital was shared by Ignatius Gennusa, clarinettist of the Baltimore Symphony, and Eugene Rousseau.

The next day started with the best line of the Workshop; Herb Couf, whom I consider the funniest man in the instrument business, giving a 9am clinic opened with: 'I know you're out there, 'cause I can hear you breathing, but I can't see you yet.' Later that day, a personal thrill was playing my own Soprano Saxophone

Concertino with the All-Eastern High School Clarinet Choir, directed by Dr Norman Heim, one of the leading figures in the Clarinet Choir movement. The evening concert was the highspot of the whole Workshop; the incomparable Phil Woods with the TSU Jazz Ensemble. Earlier in the day I sat in on the Phil Woods master class, so had gained some insight into the master's approach. Mere technical instrumental ability is taken for granted, and dismissed with the remark 'I never practise,' BUT, he spends hours sitting at the piano keyboard, alto slung round neck, exploring every conceivable harmonic implication of every chord sequence. One of Phil's epigrams which I jotted down was: 'I guess I don't dig this term 'legit saxophonist'. . . like, what am I . . . chopped liver?' However, to return to the concert; I was naturally expecting to hear great playing from Phil, but the big impact of the evening came from the student band which accompanied him. These kids had not seen Phil's charts until that afternoon, but if the whole stage had been transported to London and presented as 'The Phil Woods Big Band', it would have the reception of another Herman, Kenton or Rich Band. Much of the credit for their accomplishment must go to their director, Hank Levy, who guided them discreetly through the Woods book. Before Phil even appeared we had heard two outstanding young tenor soloists, Ellery Eskelin and Brad Collins. Later, when Phil's feet got tired, he sat down on the lead alto chair, pushing its youthful occupier to the mike in this place. Young Glen Cashman was more than equal to the occasion, and gave forth with some of the highest and fastest improvisation I've heard. Then Phil joined him for an alto dialogue which was a live demonstration of the teaching methods he had earlier discussed.

On the final day I decided to use my saxophone master class to discuss the saxophone quartet, this being the only field in which I could hope to follow Rousseau and Woods without laying an egg! Not having Pete, Chris and Dave in my baggage, I borrowed three of the guys from the band, steam still coming out of their ears from the night before. Whether Ellery Eskelin, Barry Caudill and Jerry Donato would describe themselves as 'legit' or 'chopped liver' saxophonists really didn't matter, as they read my 'charts' with as much aplomb as the Phil Woods ones, and the debut of 'The London Saxophone Quartet of Baltimore' was a great success.

Now came the time to bid farewell to the comparatively familiar Eastern Seaboard and seek my fortune in the West. I had been invited to participate in a two day Clarinet and Saxophone Symposium at North Texas State University in 'Dynamic' Denton, a small town near Dallas. My host there was Dr James Gillespie, who had planned a busy week of presymposium rehearsals with my excellent accompanist, Judy Fisher, various groups of students who were to give a concert of my works, and huge Texas-sized meals, none of which I was able to finish. In England I seem to have this image as the pear-shaped gourmand of Twickenham, but in Texas I'm just a Broken Reed in the scoffing stakes!

I had heard that NTSU has over 100 saxophone majors, the best of whom play in the nine 'Lab Bands' around which the Jazz Education programme centre. I was advised to go and hear the 1 o'clock band, which is the best, and gathered that the other eight followed daily for a one-hour rehearsal through the afternoon and into the evening. The 1 o'clock band was certainly magnificent, and I stayed on to hear some of the 2 o'clock band, just to see how less advanced it might be. But it sounded just as good to me! Then I had to leave for a rehearsal, but passing the Jazz Lab around 6pm I popped in just to see how ropey the bands were at this end of the scale. The 6 o'clock band was in full cry, and sounded just as good as that 1 o'clock band! I crept quietly away to lose myself in the succulent depths of yet another steak. This fantastic jazz education programme is supervised by Leon Breeden, a fine jazz clarinettist, whose son is principal clarinet of the San Fransisco Symphony.

Next day Gary Foster, the brilliant doubler from Los Angeles, gave the best jazz performance of the Symposium, accompanied by the 1 o'clock band rhythm section. The London Saxophone Quartet of Denton also made its debut, in which I was joined by my latest victims, Bob Seligson, Joe Eckert and Billy Rogers. Really I felt it was a shame to spoil their fine intonation and ensemble by displacing their proper soprano player, Steve Duke (pronnounced *Dook*) as the pieces they played on their own were really impressive.

So, once again, I saddled up my trusty horse and rode westwards into the sunset, heading for Tucson, Arizona. Here our very own John Denman has taken up residence as professor of Clarinet at the University of Arizona. As I got off the plane (I wasn't really on horseback) and entered the airport building I was amazed to hear the strains of 'God Save the Queen' played by a clarinet choir. Thinking I was hallucinating from excessive crossing of time zones, I was just about to head for the bar for medicinal purposes, when I saw 'Rugged John' Denman conducting the University of Arizona Clarinet Choir, all formed up for my inspection. I've never had a welcome like that before at an airport and don't suppose I ever will again! It was all very touching, and a bit like Stanley and Livingstone as the two wandering Limeys wept quietly on each other's shoulders and headed for the bar together. When I arrived at the University I realised that this was planned as the fun scene of the tour, as John had arranged 'An Evening With Paul Harvey', advertised by Brigitte Frick posters all the way from Switzerland announcing 'Hippo Harvey' and 'Uncle Paul from Kneller Hall'. Fortunately I was able to satisfy the hippo fanciers of Tucson, as Elizabeth Ervin, the saxophone professor, kindly lent me three of her Sonora Saxophone Quartet (Linda Magata, David Lopez and Jessie Sanders) for a performance of *'Saxopotamus'* with eccentric narrating soprano player, by the London Saxophone Quartet of Tucson.

I also conducted the Clarinet Choir with a chopstick, because John's baton, with which he later conducted my Soprano Concertino is the longest I've ever seen; I think he must use it to kill rattlesnakes. In fact, as I stood next to him to play the solo part, the *swish* of his first downbeat quite unnerved me for the first few bars! A highspot of this concert for me was to be accompanied by Paula Fan, affectionately known to her friends as 'Jaws 2'. Nearly all the clarinet recitals I have reviewed in recent years have been accompanied by this fine pianist. The fact that she was seized by uncontrollable hunger during my cadenza and produced a lunch box from under the piano in no way detracted from my pleasure in working with her!

After the concert a party at John's house developed into a jam session with some members of his group 'Jazzberry Jam'; Jeff Haskell (piano), Tom Ervin (trombone) and Walt St Pierre (trumpet). I must have eventually fallen asleep on a sofa, because the last I remember is Jeff, holding a bottle of bourbon, leaning over me saying, 'Jeez, the poor son of a bitch is pooped out!'

As well as these excesses, clinics at the University and Rincon High School, John had arranged several entertaining happenings for me. These included a cactus, snake and tarantula fancier's tour of the Sonora Desert Museum, a visit to Old Tucson, where *The High Chapparral* is filmed, a gigantic steak 'n' beans dinner in Traildust Town, where the waitress cuts your tie off and pins it on the ceiling (must be symbolic of something, I suppose), followed by a visit to a photographer's studio where you can dress up as any character from the Old West and be immortalised in 19th century-style sepia. As I spent much of my youth dressed up as a cowboy, I chose the more martial image of a Captain of Confederate Cavalry, complete with moustache, sword and Colt '45.

Next day I flew to Los Angeles to pick up the Polar Express flight to London. My last instance of the friendliness of the musicians of America was that the eminent clarinettist and reed designer, Mitchell Lurie, left his sick wife's bedside to drive to the airport, buy me a coffee and help me while away the time between flights with an interesting chat. I leave you with No. 179 in my American Phrasebook: 'YO'ALL HEVVA GOOD DAIY NEOW, Y'HEUH.'

Not many people know that I served as an officer of the Confederate Cavalry in Tucson, Arizona.

Jim Gillespie, John Denman and the author.

HAVE SAXOPHONE WILL TRAVEL

(Being an account of the London Saxophone Quartet's visit to the 1972 World Saxophone Congress in Toronto, Canada).

PART ONE — PROLOGUE
The World of many London musicians is bounded in the North by Elstree TV Studios (known in the trade as 'Fort Knox'); in the East by Barking Town Hall and in the West by Shepperton Film Studios. To venture beyond these confines can produce unpleasant symptoms, such as nose-bleeding, which can only be assuaged by a very thick compress of five pound notes.

The LSQ, however, believe that the medium of the saxophone quartet should be taken to as wide an audience as possible, and have ranged the length and breadth of Britain to this end. Many provincial music lovers, who hitherto thought of the saxophone as something to stuff paper hats into at New Year's Eve Dances, have been amazed to discover that the saxophone quartet is one of the most effective of all chamber music combinations.

Up to this year the furthest of these LSQ expeditions had been to Thurso, at the northern tip of Scotland, where the hardy inhabitants, were regaled with Glazounov, Pierné and Bozza, to an accompaniment of the cries of sea-birds, the barking of seals, a howling North-Westerly gale, and the grey Atlantic pounding through Pentland Firth on to the barren rocks of the Orkney Islands. When musicians are gathered in warm, womb-like recording studios, deep underground beneath the crowded streets of London, this saga is recounted with bated breath, and studio-tans grow even paler at the thought of four saxophone players being so far from the London Telephone System and the nearest reed shop.

So there we were, drinking coffee in Hale Hambleton's kitchen one raw autumn morning, trying to summon up the energy to molest a few more semiquavers, when I dropped my news like a pebble into a pond: 'There's this saxophone player in Toronto called Paul Brodie who wants us to play at this World Saxophone Congress there next August.' . . . PLOP! . . . the ripples widened . . . 'Toronto?' . . . 'that's past Shepperton' . . . past Wales' . . . 'past Ireland' . . . 'it's in Canada . . . 'over . . . the . . . ATLANTIC! . . .?!' 'Blimey,' said Dave, 'we can't go as far as that, mate, we might fall over the edge!' 'Really, Dave,' said Hale, 'haven't you heard of Christopher Columbus?' 'Columbus . . . Chris Columbus . . .,' muttered Dave, thoughtfully chewing his baritone sling, 'the name rings a bell . . . what instument does he play?'

We could hear Chris's brain humming: 'Yes... good... Canada ... new British music... export or die... Birthday Honours List ... Services to British Music... all get OBE... broadcast every day... TV every week... record every month... Royal Festival Hall used exclusively for saxophone quartet recitals (Paul... you MUST write a Concerto for saxophone quartet, twelve harps, organ, symphony orchestra and choir; its VERY urgent; we've NOTHING for that combination...)... all knighted... State Funerals all round... buried in Westminster Abbey... knock down Nelson's Column... erect enormous saxophone-shaped monument in its place in Trafalgar Square... LSQ Square, rather ... not enough new British music... we'll have a composers' competition... (see to that, please Hale...) what are we sitting here gossiping for?... We must rehearse... rehearse...'

If you latch onto the right part of the Thoughts of Chairman Chris, there is usually a sound idea to be followed up. In this case it was the Composers' Competition, and we set that in motion. Eventually my study was littered with 132 parts and 33 scores of new saxophone quartet works, not to mention numerous letters from composers, saying such things as 'Since sending you my saxophone quartet I have spent many hours in meditation and soul-searching, and have decided that the top G sharp hemidemi-semiquaver on the soprano in bar 197 of the third movement should be piano instead of mezzo piano.'

So we now had a substantial British saxophone quartet repertoire, and the only remaining chore was to finance our journey across the Atlantic. Numerous begging letters were dispatched to every conceivable organization; replies were polite, but negative. For example, The League of British Empire Loyalists replied, 'While we applaud your conviction that exposing the North American Indians to contemporary British Saxophone Quartet music would indirectly lead to the Government of the United States applying to rejoin the British Commonwealth, we are, frankly unable to follow your train of thought on this matter. We are, therefore, unable to offer you any form of grant until such time as concrete evidence of your influence in such a course of events may be forthcoming from Washington D.C.' In desperation, I decided to try selling Military Secrets to the Russians, and called at the Soviet Embassy with a microfilmed blueprint of Kneller Hall's secret weapon, the Bass Fanfare Trumpet, concealed inside a hollow tooth. I was received courteously by their Military Attache, and given a glass of vintage Mongolian sherry. He regretted, however, that the microfilm was of no value to them, as the Bass Fanfare Trumpet, he said, flicking a speck of dust from his Order of Lenin, was originally a Russian invention, anyway.

However, I felt guilty at having sunk to these depths, when the good old British Council eventually came up with the promise of a generous grant towards our fares and expenses. So, whistling *Rule Britannia* through tightly clenched teeth, we packed our sandwiches, reeds and toothbrushes, and prepared to assail the New World.

SAXODYSSEY, 1973

An account of the London Saxophone Quartet's visit to Spain and the Corfu Festival.

So there we were once again at Heathrow Airport, about to embark on another saga of Gradwell Tours Inc. Check-in scales groaned protestingly under the weight of the tenor and baritone ... excess baggage tickets showered upon us like confetti ... metal detectors went berserk with whirring dials and flashing lights when confronted with Adolphe Sax's brain child ... anti-hijacking guards poked suspicious fingers up the bell of my soprano to find the bullets and firing mechanism ... but all this is the daily routine of anyone rash enough to hurtle around the skies of the world with a saxophone quartet.

Eventually we were in the air, heading southwest for Santiago de Compostela, Spain. Hale Hambleton was not with us on this trip, being chained by the ankle to the first clarinet stand in the pit at Sadlers Wells Opera, where the first production of Wagner's 'Ring' in English was about to erupt. In his place, on alto, was Anton Weinberg (hereafter referred to as Tony), recently escaped from the dark recesses of the BBC's Birmingham studios and now making a name (even if nobody can spell it) for himself in London as a multi-woodwind doubler. His studio pallor was beginning to wear off and his eyes glinted through his rimless glasses with new hope and expectation of the new life ahead.

Chris sits tense, expectant, wearing his intrepid birdman expression, awaiting his moment of glory. He has a pilot's licence, you see, and is waiting for the stewardess to emerge, white-faced, from the flight cabin to say, 'Both the pilots are unconscious from food poisoning. Does anyone on board know how to fly a plane?' It happens so often in movies; Chris never gives up hope.

Dave sits morosely chewing his baritone sling, waiting for the plane to plummet into the sea like a stone. He steadfastly refuses to believe that a big metal thing like an aeroplane can fly through the air, and is convinced that the whole thing is some elaborate confidence trick. Readers have written to ask me whether Dave wears his baritone sling in bed. The answer is no; he takes it off and soaks it overnight in a glass of whisky, which is why he chews it in moments of stress.

Fortunately, these hopes and fears once again came to nothing in an uneventful flight, and we were soon in two taxis, speeding through the Spanish countryside towards La Coruna, spraying clouds of dust over the native population, which appeared to consist exclusively of old ladies, dressed in black, leading cows.

Next day, in the Hotel Atlantico, came the first, and worst crisis. It is routine to expect some dents and scrapes in the tenor and baritone from the dainty handling of the airport baggage men. But none of us were prepared for the misshapen travesty of a tenor saxophone which emerged from Chris's case. We knew the top of a saxophone bends towards the player, but we'd never seen one before where the main body of the instrument bent sideways as well. Chris was screaming, 'Ring up Selmers in Madrid; they'll have to fly another tenor up here' . . . I was frantically composing the Spanish for 'We cannot the concert tonight give; the tenor saxophone he is broken' . . . Dave had swallowed the hook of his baritone sling and was quietly choking in a corner. It's at moments like this that a cool-headed, clear-thinking man can emerge as a natural leader. In a flash Tony became the man of the moment. 'Come on, Paul,' he yelled, charging into the corridor, 'we need a long piece of wood.' There was a maid sweeping the floor; 'That'll do; what's the Spanish for broom?' 'No idea,' I said, snatching the broom from the terrified maid; 'Por favor, senorita, el broomo un momentito, muchas gracias.' A moment later Tony was thrusting the broomstick down the body of the tenor . . . hold it steady . . . bang . . . bang . . . it's straight . . . screwdriver . . . pliers . . . cigarette lighter . . . flame here . . . now there . . . cigarette paper . . . more heat . . . screwdriver . . . In ten minutes, steely eyes narrow slits peering through the rimless glasses, hands steady and sure as a surgeon in the emergency operating theatre, Tony had reseated every pad at the top of the instrument. We sat, bathed in sweat, trembling with disbelief as Chris put the mouthpiece on and ran down to bottom B flat . . . and up . . . and down . . . soft . . . loud . . . everything worked. WOODWIND WORLD SALUTES ANTON WEINBERG — the guy to have around in a crisis!

At 11pm that evening we gave our first concert in the beautiful old Church of the Third Order of St Francis; part of a Festival called 'Nights in the Old City'. I had taken it upon myself to introduce the programme in Spanish, and was delighted to find that the capacity audience not only appeared to understand what I said, but even laughed at the jokes. It's very difficult to be funny in a foreign language; mind you, the Spanish are an extremely kind and polite race but they must have understood enough to know they were supposed to be jokes, I suppose. Another medal for Tony; as well as fitting in brilliantly with the saxophone quartet, he also played bassoon with Dave and Chris on clarinets, in a Mozart Divertimento in each of the concerts.

We gave one more concert in La Coruna the following evening, and next day were in the air again, bound for Barcelona. Here we recorded two television recitals in the extravagantly rococo Palacio de Musica part of a series called 'Grandes Interpradores'. Spanish TV producers like to record the whole programme non-stop, and having played the first 25-minute recital, they informed us that the tape had broken in the middle, and we'd have to do it all again. A highspot for viewers must be where I'm playing a long solo in Frank Cordell's *Patterns* and a big fat fly settles on my bell and crawls into the B hole. I was oblivious to this drama, but the others were watching, fascinated, to see what might happen if I played that note. Luckily the solo is all at the top of the instrument.

Next day, Ulysses Gradwell and his merrie men took to the air again, over the wine dark sea, for Greece and its enchanted Isle of Corfu. The playing we enjoyed most there was a series of informal concerts in a beautiful old square in the ancient town of Corfu, the island's capital. We stood around a medieval carved plinth in the middle of the square and played all our lighter selections to a highly appreciative audience of the local inhabitants, including dozens of wide-eyed children of all ages, sitting on the ground in well-behaved rows. In the intervals, residents of the surrounding houses brought us dishes of figs and drinks. The people of Corfu are very interested in wind instruments, having a thriving Town Band, which can be heard most evenings, rehearsing in a room over a taverna.

Eventually we were airborne again, heading back to England. That same evening we gave a concert in the crypt of St Martin-in-the-Fields Church, Trafalgar Square. We enjoyed playing, because the acoustics are very flattering and the temperature was about 30 degrees cooler than Corfu. The quaint, lovable inhabitants of London were appreciative and well-behaved, but nobody brought us a dish of figs in the interval!

Paul Brodie, Eminent Canadian Saxophonist, and host of the 1972 World Saxophone Congress in Toronto. He is pictured with Paul Harvey at the latter's Twickenham home, trying out some of his extensive collection of soprano saxophones.

Church of Third Order of St. Francis, La Coruna, Spain, July 1973.

TOURS WITH THE BBC SYMPHONY ORCHESTRA

Somewhere in the USA, 1965. Pierre Boulez is in the foreground.

Outside the Philharmonic Hall in Leningrad, USSR. USSR Tour, 1967 (Burrrr!)

THE LONDON SAXOPHONE QUARTET IN THE MIDDLE EAST

The life of an itinerant saxophone quartet is often one of sharp contrast, but none more so than twenty-four hours in the life of the LSQ some weeks ago. We finished a short Northern tour in the Lake District, drove back to London after the concert, had a few hours sleep, and were off to Heathrow next morning. Soon we were being squirted through the aluminium tubes of Charles de Gaulle airport, crossing Paris to Orly, and approximately twenty-four hours after the Lake District concert were standing beneath the palm trees of Algiers. After catching up on some sleep in the faded French colonial opulence of the St Georges Hotel, which was Allied HQ during the war, we emerged next day to record a programme in the mild chaos of the Algerian TV studios and to give our first concert. The British Council Library turned out to have the best acoustics we were to encounter on the whole tour, so it helped us to a good start. French being the second language after Arabic in North Africa, I mangled my tonsils around the introductions in O level patois, which always improves the atmosphere, however bad the grammar.

Next day we were winging across the Atlas mountains and the Sahara Desert to Tunis, our first stay of any length. The contrast is quite noticeable; Algiers has a somewhat iron-curtainish atmosphere, and the transition to Tunis is like East Berlin (with palm trees) to Paris (with palm trees). Pavement cafes abound, and we played in the Conservatoire de Musique, where solfege exercises come from every window, occasionally surprising the Western ear with the insertion of the odd quarter tone. This fusion is the main policy of the Tunis Conservatoire, and for years the staff have been grappling with the problems of writing out Arabic songs with Western notation. As most readers will probably know, musical notation goes from left to right. But Arabic words go from right to left ... Problem! Write the music backwards? Turn the word upside down?. The current compromise is to write each Arabic syllable right to left, but have the syllables running left to right to fit the music. Any reader with a better solution should contact Tunis Conservatoire immediately, where a brilliant new career awaits him.

There is an English composer on the staff, Daniel Scott-Maddocks. Seven years ago he planned a violin recital tour of Africa and arranged to meet his accompanist in Tunis. For some reason the pianist never showed up, and Dan is still there, teaching at the Conservatoire and playing the organ at Tunis RC

Cathedral. He wrote a saxophone quartet piece especially for our visit, which we played at both the Tunis concerts.

A few days later we were off to the Gulf (Persian or Arabian, depending where your political sympathies lie), breaking our journey in Beirut amidst the bullet holes and broken windows of the war-scarred airport. Now for a taste of the real Arab world, I thought, as we checked into the Omar Khayyam Hotel in Bahrain. Beneath my window a herd of goats made a hearty meal of cardboard boxes on a picturesque rubbish dump. Across the potholed street the local mosque stretched its slim tower to the steel blue sky. 'A Muezzin from the Tower of Darkness cries . . .' But no longer, I fear. Nowadays the Muezzin sits downstairs in the mosque in front of the microphone, and PA loudspeakers protrude from the tower, beneath the neon lights, calling the faithful to prayer. Some mosques even use tape recordings, I was told! Pausing only to slap a 'KEEP MUSIC LIVE' sticker on the mosque, I moved on, a sadder and wiser traveller. One point in Bahrain's favour; here we actually saw our only real live camels. Driving through the desert to the Bahrain TV station, a free range herd undulated sneeringly across the road to disappear in a cloud of greyish sand.

In Kuwait I appreciated the reason for the Muezzins' amplified prayers. Every mosque stands beside a six-lane highway. The characteristic sound of the Middle East is the motor horn. The Arab motorist uses his horn as if it were a vital part of the car's propulsion, like the accelerator. Omar's muezzin would stand about as much chance against the Cadillacs of Kuwait as a clavichord in the 1812 Overture! (Now I'm back in London, the hardest thng to adjust to is the eerie silence in the streets as I drive around the West End). Here we did a concert in an oil town. In my ignorance this venue conjured up an expectation of corrugated iron shacks inhabited by oil-smeared John Wayne-type drill pushers. In reality an oil town is like a suburb of Cheltenham, planted incongruously in the middle of the desert. Kuwait being officially opposed to the three curses of Islam, alcohol, tobacco and unveiled women, the country is dry. Yet human nature being what it is, more drinking takes place in the oil town than Glasgow on a Saturday night. In each trim villa lurks an illicit still for the manufacture of 'flash'; a vodka-type spirit, to which is added gin or whisky flavouring. An American engineer having recently blown up himself and his house, the oil companies now issue their employees with a booklet on how to make flash safely.

So we left the Gulf for Baghdad, ancient capital of Iraq. Just for a one-night stand; we missed out on the other thousand! Again that iron-curtainish atmosphere, which would hardly have suited Ali Baba. A rather strange concert in the University; as we started to play, half the quartet were dismayed to see about 50 people get up and leave. But the other half of the quartet, facing the other side of the hall, saw another fifty come in and sit down. So it continued throughout the concert, the audience maintaining about the same numbers, with continual deductions and additions. At one point the Minister of Culture got up and made an impassioned appeal in Arabic requesting the audience to promenade more quietly, but with little effect. The reason for all this appeared to be that the girl students had to be back in the Halls of Residence by certain times, or be locked out, and the boys were coming in from various late classes.

So to our final port of call, Amman, the capital of Jordan. At 2,500 feet, the air is invigorating and refreshing after the Gulf. The narrow streets wind precipitously up and down the several hills on which the town is built. Two concerts and a TV recording were our final musical duties of the tour. At a press conference I was reminded of the division between Arab and European cultures. One local reporter asked, 'Vy you got no drums?' 'Well, er,' I replied, 'a string quartet doesn't have drums, does it, so why should we?' The reporter thought about this for a moment, and then delivered the punch line of the tour:

'VATS A STRINK QUARTET?'

Collapse of stout infidel!

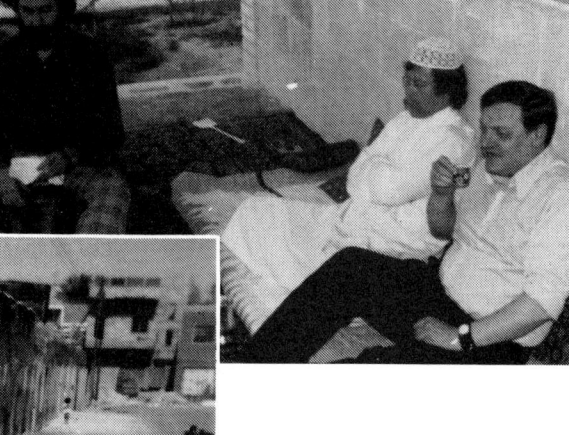

Pete Ripper, Kuwait British Council representative (he'd gone native!) and the author.

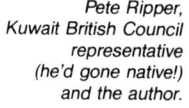

This was the view from our hotel!

The author with goat in Bahrain.   The LSQ in Souk.

In the Arabian Gulf.

A VISIT TO THE BUFFET FACTORY
WITH THE LONDON SAXOPHONE QUARTET

... or at least three-quarters of it ...

Actually, it was nearly only a half of it, because Peter Ripper couldn't come owing to BBC commitments, and Dave Lawrence missed the plane. Alan Lucas (Buffet's UK representative), John Coppen (senior instrument technician at Pages Walk), Chris Gradwell, and myself took off at 9am leaving Dave's ticket and the address of the hotel at the Air France departure desk.

Arriving panting at Heathrow to see us taking off into the sunrise, Dave embarked on a saga too harrowing to describe in a family magazine such as this. Suffice it to say that his full story has all the elements of a jet-set musician's nightmare, the only missing ingredient being that he did not lose his trousers, and his baritone was not stolen, though several people sat on it, of course.

Meanwhile, the rest of us had landed in a snow covered landscape at Charles de Gaulle, and were oozing through those surrealist tubes once more, muttering 'Dave will make it; he always does!' The airport bus took us to the terminal at Porte Maillot where Roland Kurz, the Managing Director of Buffet, had arranged to meet us. By this time a full scale blizzard was in progress and all the traffic seemed to be jammed solid. We passed the time by having lunch — typical Parisian light snack, which took about three hours to eat, by which time Roland had fought his way through the snow to us. We then set off in Roland's car for Orgeval, where the nearest hotel to the Buffet factory is. It's about twenty miles out of Paris, but the Route Nationale was jammed with skidding lorries and blue nosed gendarmes with frozen whistles, so we had to find another route round the back of Versailles.

Eventually, we reached Orgeval, checked into the hotel, and had a go at ringing Dave's home near London to see if there was any news. The nearest we got was Ballymena, Northern Ireland, where nobody had seen him so we gave up and went shopping instead. On our return to the hotel, we observed what appeared to be a dilapidated polar bear slumped in the bar, holding a glass of beer in one hand and a baritone saxophone in the other. Could it be?... Yes it was! Another three-hour dinner enlivened by Dave's account of his adventures rounded off an eventful day.

Next morning, we were at the Buffet factory in Mantes soon after 8am. The hours flew by as little men in overalls and berets, the obligatory Gauloise hanging from the lower lip, ran about measuring the height of Dave's embouchure from the floor, squinting into the octave holes of my soprano, and gesticulating wildly over Chris' tenor. Over all this activity presided the dignified Robert Carre, Buffet's chief design consultant, of RC model clarinet fame. After due deliberation over each problem, a minion was dispatched to the workshops to carry out the great man's instructions, returning in due course to present it for his inspection.

When Dave said he found the little finger action on his baritone rather heavy, M. Carre snapped his fingers like Abanazer, and declaimed, 'Let the prototype of the new model baritone be brought for Monsieur's delectation!' Pattering little French feet disappeared to some inner sanctum and returned reverently bearing an unplated baritone, naked and heat-scarred, like an embryonic Phoenix newly risen from some primeval volcano. A quick *Flight of the Bumble Bee* round bottom C-sharp to A, and Dave was moaning and gibbering with pleasure. The prototype had to be wrested from his feverish grasp by force, while M. Carre patiently explained that they had to finish it before he could take it away.

After lunch, Roland took us on a tour of the factory; fascinating to follow the progress of a block of wood and a sheet of metal through the multitude of skillful operations which result in the finished instrument we know so well.

Soon it was time to drive back to Paris where we had a tea appointment with Daniel Deffayet. Le Maitre was in fine form, and gave me a quick demonstration of soprano harmonics, from which it appeared not to matter what fingering he used, but the note he thought of always came out. I can't understand why this doesn't work for me; perhaps my eyebrows aren't bushy enough. he also regaled us with tales of his early days playing 'le baryton hot' at Le Moulin Rouge, Les Follies Bergeres, and Le Club 'Fred'. But all too soon it was time to make for the airport again to start the journey home.

Dave rounded off the story well by leaving his overnight bag behind at the Buffet factory. If any reader has recently bought a gleaming new Buffet saxophone and been bewildered to find a tatty old grip, containing a toothbrush with most of the bristles missing, a pair of pink pyjamas and a bottle of brown ale, stuffed down the bell, Buffet wishes to make it clear that this is not their latest free offer travelling saxophonist kit, provided as a standard extra with all new saxophones! Please send it back to Dave Lawrence, c/o LSQ.

SUMMER IN SEATTLE
The 1986 Conference of the International Clarinet Society

As Michel Bryant and I were the only British CASS members at this year's ICS Conference, I feel I should provide a brief report of the four days. I've written about so many of these events, clarinet, saxophone and woodwind generally, over the past fifteen years or so, that I've long since given up trying to mention everybody who played, as that becomes merely a transcript of the programme. The technique I've evolved consists of waiting a few days for the jet lag to subside and then writing down what I can remember, without referring to the programme, or worrying about who will be upset if I don't mention them.

I'd already been in Seattle for a week before the Conference started, and the weather had been rather chilly and cloudy, just like England. But on the first day of the Conference the sun came out, and the beautiful University of Washington campus was seen to its best advantage, with green vistas stretching away towards majestic snow capped Mount Ranier on the horizon. (So much for creative writing; lets get on to the music!)

I think that if everybody who was present at the Mozart Gala on the Friday evening were asked what was the musical highspot of the Conference, I'm pretty sure they would be unanimous, and that's not a statement I'd often make with much certainty! Their choice would not be some amazing new work, not some stunning display of technical virtuosity, but a simple, direct and utterly moving performance of the Mozart Quintet. It must be forty years since I first heard the work, played by Thurston or Kell (I forget which was first) but that evening in Seattle I heard the nearest possible to a perfect performance given by Mitchell Lurie with the Philadelphia String Quartet, led by the lovely young Japanese violinist Mayumi Ohira. More than a few hard boiled old-pro clarinettist were observed to be in tears, and even my English stiff upper lip was seen to quiver on occasions, I'm told!

The other group which was the most interesting to me personally, was the New World Basset Horn Trio, consisting of Eric Hoepric, Lisa Klevit and William McColl (the Conference organiser) playing on replicas of early 19th century basset horns (the bent in the middle sort). They played the Mozart Nocturnes for voices and basset horns on the Mozart Gala, and also gave a morning performance of two of the Mozart Divertimenti. Everyone who heard them was impressed by the rich sonority and excellent intonation they achieved.

At the Conferences such as this I hope to learn a lot from the clinics, and, being particularly interested in the extraneous sizes of clarinets, I was given very good value by Peter Hadcock of the Boston Symphony, author of that fine book of E flat orchestral studies, and by Dennis Smylie, one of New York's leading exponents of bass and contrabass clarinets.

The Saturday night Jazz Gala made nonsense of the sometimes heard statement that the clarinet is no longer a viable voice in jazz. One of our more successful exports to the USA, Mr John Denman, started it going, and I swear that he's been practising again since I last heard him play jazz! Every time I see him I implore him not to practise any more, otherwise where will it all end, I ask myself?

Then came Japan's answer to Benny Goodman; Eiji Kitamura; a gentleman of great personal charm and refined musical taste. All the ladies in the audience wanted to cuddle him, and the clarinettists wanted to break his fingers! (That would make a good quote for his write-up book!)

Third on was the legendary Bill Smith, alter ego of William O. Smith, Professor of Composition at the University of Washington. I'm not generally a fan of electronics, but the tasteful way Bill uses them to enhance his wonderfully inventive jazz improvisation really had me won over.

'Well,' I remarked to my companion in the intermission, 'I don't care if I WERE Buddy De Franco, and had to follow those three, I think I'd just go round to the pub, forget the whole thing and LEAVE them to it!'

But Mr De Franco is made of sterner stuff than I, needless to say, and, not a wit dismayed, DID follow them with his usual demonstration of the style which laid the foundations of modern jazz clarinet playing, on which he has been building ever since.

These are my main recollections of the Conference, but I was also fortunate to be able to enjoy some fine performances before and after the four days, at the Olympic Music Festival, a short ferry voyage across Puget Sound, in the idyllic setting of a farm owned by Alan Iglitzin, viola player of the Philadelphia Quartet.

One of the guest artists this season was Kathleen Jones, principal clarinet of the Puerto Rico Symphony, who gave three notable chamber music performances in the course of the festival; the Brahms Quintet with the Philadelphia Quartet, the Beethoven Trio and the Brahms Trio with Bonnie Hampton (cello) and

Nathan Schwartz (piano), a fine husband and wife duo from San Fransisco.

In the past I've been accused of not being much impressed by anything that happens outside Twickenham, but now I'll come right out and say it, folks . . . For two weeks this summer, Seattle had Twickenham beat to a frazzle all along the line!

Paul Harvey in his erstwhile capacity as visiting Basset Horn clinician at El Conservatorio De Musica, San Juan, Puerto Rico. The trouble is, my regular readers always think this is a joke, because I have so often referred to my friends as 'Professor of Basset Horn at Pease Pottage Polytechnic', etc.

A classic case of 'cry wolf', I'm afraid, because I really did go there six times in all; only once with the basset horn, admittedly, other times with soprano and alto sax or clarinet.

It's not easy, folks, trying to talk about basset horn fingerings in South American Spanish, remembering not to use the 'stuck-up' Castilian accent you learnt at school. I must admit, it's been quite a relief to get back to 'Dos cervezas, por favor!'

3 Hippos and Humour

THE BIZARRE CULT OF THE HIPPOPOTAMUS

How on earth did it all start? I THINK, when my daughter was little, and just starting to learn French, we watched a Jacques Cousteau programme on TV, showing underwater films of hippos. M. Cousteau kept describing them in his infectious French accent, as 'ZEE 'EEPPOS', and somehow, we came to think of the Hippo as a French, instead of African animal. Then I had to write something for narrator and saxophone quartet for Children's Concerts, and as we always started off by describing the instruments and their invention, I decided to develop this theme, and so Hippolyte Saxopotamus was born, living in some parallel world where Nineteenth Century Paris was populated entirely by French Hippos, who are obviously the lords of creation; I suppose human beings were rolling in the mud in African lakes!

I also definitely remember my daughter saying once that all my drawings of people looked like hippos, anyway, so I decided to specialise in hippos for my naive art activities. The Hippodeus String Quartet, Dame Lily Potamus and the Hippobethan Consort were actually commissioned for an exhibition put on by Concert Agents for Chamber Music Societies.

SAXOPOTAMUS

Hippolyte Saxopotamus was FURIOUS. 'Where eez my screwdriver?' he shouted, stamping up and down his workshop. 'Jean-Paul . . . Jean-Paul . . .' Where WAS that wretched apprentice . . . never there when he was needed . . . had he forgotten that tomorrow was the great day when his master was to demonstrate his new invention, the piece de resistance of the Maison Saxopotamus, the mighty Contrabass Hippophone, to the Emperor himself?

General Leboue, Commander in Chief of all the French Army Bands had sent for Hippolyte several months ago, and instructed him to invent the most spectacular wind instrument the world had ever seen, which would make French Army Bands the envy of all other countries. 'La France looks to you, Monsieur Saxopotamus,' he had said, 'Eef your invention pleases ze Empereur zere weel be a legion d'Honneur for you, and a beeg Military contract.'

And now, with the honour of France hanging in the balance, not to mention the good name of Maison Saxopotamus, his work was being held up by that lazy, good for nothing boy . . . 'JEAN-PAUL . . . JEAN-PAUL . . .'

At last a small grubby face peeped around the door. 'Eer I am, M'sieu,' squeaked the apprentice, a diminutive hippopotamus, about twelve years old, wearing an extremely dirty apron, and carrying an even dirtier piece of rag and a tin of brass polish.

'Where eez my screwdriver?' screamed Hippolyte.

'Stuck behind your ear, M'sieu,' replied Jean-Paul.

'Well, why were you not eere to tell me so when I needed you, wretched boy?' shouted Hippolyte, feeling rather silly as he pulled the screwdriver from behind his ear and started tightening up the hundreds of screws on the monstrous instrument on his workbench. Jean-Paul watched his master at work, dreaming of the day when he himself would be a famous inventor of musical instruments, entertaining great composers and musicians in his workshop. Every so often his reverie would be interrupted as Hippolyte shouted, 'Where eez the pliers?' or 'Where eez the oilcan?' or 'Where eez the soldering iron?' and Jean-Paul would scurry here and there around the workshop fetching them. At last Hippolyte gave a final twist to the final screw, and with a great sigh laid down his screwdriver. 'So . . .' he breathed, 'the contrabasss Hippophone, she is finished. Now, my boy, comes your part. I am going to bed now, as I will need all my strength in the morning, to blow this masterpiece. But you must polish the brass until it shines like new.

Now, Jean-Paul had spent most of his young life polishing brass instruments, but never before had he tackled such a monster as this. On and on through the night he polished, in and out the curls and twists of tubing, up and down the valves, round and round the great brass body . . . at last he had finished the outside . . . but the Emperor might look inside the enormous bell . . . M'sieu

Saxopotamus certainly would, anyway, so he took his rag and tin of polish, and crawled into the bell . . .

At eight next morning Hippolyte came into the workshop wearing his best frockcoat. 'Jean-Paul, Jean-Paul,' he shouted. The wretched boy was nowhere to be seen; well, at least he had polished the hippophone well, for it shone like a mirror in the morning sun. Hippolyte ran outside into Rue Lepic and called a cab. If the boy was not to be found he would just have to miss the visit to the Palace. The cab driver, cursing and sweating, helped Hippolyte carry the hippophone out of the workshop and strap it on top of the cab. 'To ze Palace of ze Empereur, my good man,' shouted Hippolyte at the top of his voice, so that all his neighbours would hear, and spread the word throughout Montmartre that the mad inventor of Rue Lepic had gone to see the Emperor.

At last Hippolyte found himself waiting in the throne room, enveloped in the coils of the hippophone, and surrounded by all the Bandmasters of the French Army, and several important composers and conductors. Suddenly there was a flourish of trumpets, and a voice shouted, 'EEZ IMPERIAL MAJESTEE . . . NAPOLEON HIPPOPARTE . . .' This was the moment when Hippolyte was to play *The Marseillaise*, so he took a gigantic breath . . . and . . . BLEWWWWWWWWWW . . . Nothing! He took another even more gigantic breath, and BLEWWWWWWWWWWW . . . Still nothing. The Emperor was looking at him, quizzically . . . the Bandmasters were clearing their throats in embarrassment . . . General Leboue was glaring at him . . . He took the biggest breath of his life, and BLEWWWWWWWWWWWW and out of the bell shot a diminutive hippopotamus, wearing a filthy apron, clutching in one hand an even filthier rag and in the other a nearly empty tin of brass polish. This apparition sailed through the air, and landed at the feet of the Emperor. Jean-Paul, for of course, it was none other, opened one sleepy eye, squeaked, 'Vive L'Empereur!' and started polishing the Imperial boots with his filthy piece of rag.

There was a deathly silence in the throne room. Suddenly the Emperor recovered from his surprise . . . his eyes twinkled, and he grinned then chuckled . . . he laughed . . . and laughed . . . everybody laughed. Then the Emperor held up his hand for silence, and lifted Jean-Paul to his feet and embraced him. 'I have often wondered who it was who polished the new brass instruments which Monsieur Saxopotamus sends to the Band of the Garde Hippocaine,' he said, 'Now I know.' And everybody cheered.

'Monsieur Saxopotamus,' continued the Emperor, 'now that

you have cleared the obstruction from your magnificent invention, perhaps you would care to let us hear if it sounds as marvellous as it looks.' Hippolyte bowed as well as the coils of hippophone would permit, and started to play *The Marseillaise*. The sonorous notes shook the very foundations of the Palace, and courtiers, bandmasters and Generals alike gasped in admiration. Amidst the cheers and 'Bravos' which followed the last mighty note, the Emperor stepped forward and hung the coveted sash of the Legion of Honour around Hippolyte's neck. Putting his arm around Jean-Paul's shoulder, he again called for silence.

'Unfortunately this industrious young hippo is too young to be a Companion of the Legion of Honour, but I hereby appoint him Honorary Polisher of all Brass Instruments to all the Bands of the Imperial Guard.'

Later that day, after a sumptuous banquet, Hippolyte and Jean-Paul returned to Montmartre. As their cab turned the corner from Place Blanche, the whole of Rue Lepic welcomed them with cheers and cries of 'Vive L'Hippophone ... Vive Jean-Paul.'

Back inside the workshop at last, Hippolyte sank exhausted into his threadbare armchair. Jean-Paul went into the kitchen to make some cocoa. Suddenly a voice form the workshop shouted, 'Jean-Paul ... where eez my pencil ... where eez my ruler ... where eez my drawing paper ...?' Hippolyte Saxopotamus had had another idea!

The Hippodeus String Quartet.

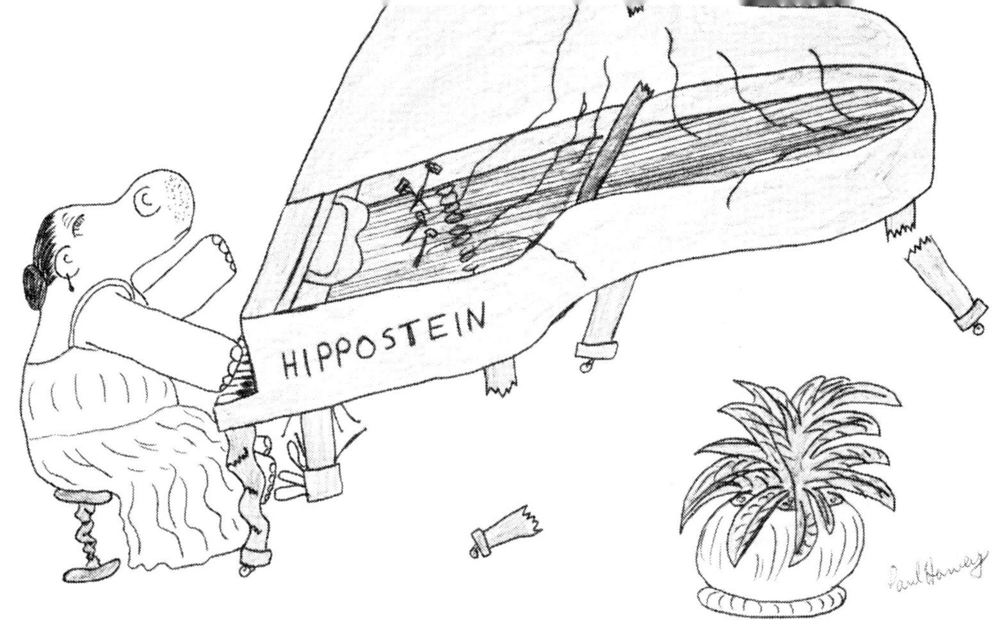

Dame Lily Potamus at the climax of a memorable recital.

The Hippobethan Consort.

39

The London Hippophone Quartet.

The LHQ on tour.

The New York Hippophone Quartet rehearsing in their Manhatten penthouse.

The Riverside Saxophone Quartet — drawn after taking my daughter to see Toad of Toad Hall.

THE SINGULAR AFFAIR OF THE FABERGÉ MOUTHPIECE

By Dr John H. Watson
Assisted by Sir Arthur Conan Doyle and Paul Harvey

PART I: AN UNUSUAL VISITOR

The yellow November fog swirled across Baker Street as I stared from the bow window of 221b. Behind me my friend, Sherlock Holmes, sprawled in an armchair, aimlessly drawing his violin bow across a foul-smelling pipe. With a sigh of boredom he absently took a handful of shag tobacco from a Persian slipper, and stuffed it into his violin. 'Dear me, Watson,' he grunted, 'I fear the criminal element of London is as inactive as we are in this inclement season.' 'Wait,' I replied, 'I fancy we are about to receive a visitor,' for at that moment a hansom cab, its oil lamps lit against the gloom, although the hour was but two in the afternoon, pulled up at the kerb, and I observed its occupant toss half a sovereign to the driver and pull violently at our doorbell.

'How singular, Holmes,' I said, 'If you were not sitting here before my eyes, I would swear it was you who emerged from that hansom!' Before I had time to elaborate upon my reasons for this observation, Mrs Hudson had admitted our visitor, who could now be heard bounding up the stairs two at a time. As he burst into the room we perceived why, at a distance, he could be taken for Holmes, being clad in an exact replica of the costume habitually affected by my friend; voluminous ulster cape and deerstalker hat. At close quarters, however, he was seen to be shorter and more thick-set, and when he spoke it was immediately apparent that he was an American, and a greatly agitated one at that.

'Mr Holmes, Dr Watson, pray forgive this unseemly intrusion upon your privacy, but I must consult you upon a matter of the utmost gravity.'

'A moment, sir,' said Holmes, helping our visitor off with his cape. 'Pray be seated and compose yourself. I perceive that you are by profession a player of the alto saxophone, passing through London on your way home to New York after a tour of Russia.' The stranger's face broke into an infectious grin: 'Of course you are correct in every respect, Mr Holmes. I have long been an avid reader of Dr Watson's chronicles of your cases. As you would say, I know your methods. Undoubtedly, as you helped me off with my coat, you observed the label bearing the name of a Manhattan tailor, and also a Russian cloakroom ticket still pinned inside.

'The mark on the back of my collar is indicative of a saxophone sling, confirmed by the configuration of my facial muscles and the calloused groove in my right thumb. You deduce that the alto is my speciality from the position of the shiny patch on the inside of my right trouser leg where the bell rubs. Were I a tenor player it would be on the outside of the right leg.'

'Great heavens, Holmes,' I exclaimed. 'You have met your match at last.' 'Touche, Watson,' chuckled Holmes, with a rueful smile. 'I am tempted to regale our American friend with the story of my youthful sojourn in Paris. I had lodgings in the Rue Myrha, and amused myself by designing a new wind instrument with a single reed mouthpiece and a conical metal bore. I entrusted the blueprints to a Belgian instrument maker who had a small atelier next door, for him to make a prototype. I was about to patent it under the name 'Holmesophone', when urgent business called me back to London ... but all that is irrelevant to our present enquiry ... pray tell us your name, sir, and how I may be of service to you.'

PART II: THE AMERICAN'S NARRATIVE

Our visitor cleared his throat and began: 'My name is Albert Regni, and I have the honour to be a member of the New York Saxophone Quartet. Years of study at the Eastman School and the Manhattan School of Music brought me to this exalted position. I have played with many great symphony orchestras, including a tour of Japan with the New York Philharmonic, and have even recorded with the Modern Jazz Quartet.' ('What is Jazz?' I muttered. 'Be quiet, Watson,' snapped Holmes). Regni continued: 'I am now on the faculties of Kingsborough College and the State of New York at Purchase. The leader of our quartet is Raymond Beckenstein, a top New York studio musician. He has recorded with every well-known band, including Goodman and Shaw, and also works with the New York Philharmonic and the American Symphony Orchestra.

'Our tenor player is David Tofani, who studied at Juilliard under Joseph Allard. ('Ah, dear old Joe,' murmured Holmes. 'Be quiet, Holmes,' I snapped). Besides much prestigious symphony work, he is a member of the National Jazz Ensemble, and is on the faculty of Manhattan School of Music.

'Walter Kane has recently joined us on the baritone. His experiences are equally wide-ranging, and he is involved with several television shows, mainly the very successful *Sesame Street*. ('What is television?' asked Holmes and I in unison. 'Be quiet, gentlemen,' snapped Regni).

'On this recent Russian tour we visited St Petersburg, and were commanded to play before the Tsar of all the Russias at the Winter Palace. After the performance His Majesty presented our leader, Raymond Beckenstein, with a soprano mouthpiece inlaid with rubies by the court jeweller, Fabergé. We returned across Europe, reached London, and when Raymond opened his soprano case at the hotel . . . the Fabergé mouthpiece was gone . . . and in its place lay . . . this . . .' So saying he drew from his pocket a small black object which I took to be a very ordinary saxophone mouthpiece, such as may be purchased in any music store for a few shillings. Holmes examined it closely through his powerful lens, exclaiming several times, and scraping something off it onto a microscope slide. He then sniffed at it for some time, nodding to himself.

At last he seemed satisfied, and, seizing paper, pen and ink, scribbled a note which he sealed in an envelope.

'Perhaps you gentlemen would be kind enough to leave me with my scientific apparatus and reference books for an hour or two. Watson, I'm sure Mr Regni would enjoy tea at the Café Royal. On your way would you be so kind as to drop this note in at Scotland Yard for Inspector Lestrade. We will meet here at six, by which time I hope to have the information to lay this scoundrel by the heels... and Watson... bring your service revolver... there may be some danger.'

PART III: DENOUEMENT IN MIDDLESEX

When we returned at six, Holmes was already waiting in a hansom outside our rooms. 'Waterloo Station, cabbie,' he called as we jumped in. Lestrade was waiting for us at the ticket barrier of a suburban line, and no sooner were we seated in a First Class compartment than the train began to move. Holmes sat in a corner, chin sunk onto his chest, eyes closed, and I knew better than to disturb his reverie with inquiries as to our destination or our purpose there. Although the fog was thickening fast, I observed from the names of stations through which we passed that we were proceeding Westwards out of the Metropolis, following the course of the River Thames. After about twenty minutes we pulled in to Twickenham. Holmes leaped to his feet, flung open the carriage door and jumped down onto the platform. We hastened to keep up with him as he left the station and turned into a narrow street of mean dwellings, the few gas lamps casting but a faint glow in the thick blanket of fog rolling up from the nearby river. Suddenly, I became aware of a strange wailing noise like a soul in torment, which grew louder with every step.

Not since the awful baying of the Hound of the Baskervilles had I heard such a blood-curdling sound. 'Great heavens, Regni,' I said to my companion, 'What in the world can that be?' I saw his homely features pale in the gloom, and heard his teeth chattering. Before he could reply we had reached the house from which the sound emanated. Through a gap in the curtain a bizarre scene met our eyes. A fat, shabbily dressed man sat at a table, blowing a soprano saxophone. On the table were scattered dozens of mouthpieces, hundreds of reeds, knives, razor blades and pieces of sandpaper.

'In you go, Lestrade,' hissed Holmes. Lestrade shouted, 'In the name of the law,' kicking the door open, 'It is my duty to warn you that anything you say will be taken down and used in evidence against you.'

The fat man leaped to his feet with a terrible cry; as he pulled the mouthpiece from his instrument I saw the fiery gleam of rubies in the gaslight.

'It's mine, I tell you,' he screamed. 'If only I could find the right reed I would sound just as good as Beckenstein.'

Lestrade and I seized the struggling man, and Holmes prised the mouthpiece from his tightly clenched hand. In a moment Lestrade had the handcuffs on him and had dragged him out to a waiting police wagon.

'Well, Regni,' said Holmes, holding the ruby encrusted mouthpiece up to the light: 'Our case appears to have reached a satisfactory conclusion.'

'But Mr Holmes,' stammered Regni, 'That man . . . isn't it . . . wasn't he . . .?'

'Yes,' sighed Holmes, 'You must have recognised him. A tragic case; quite mad now, I fear . . .'

'But who is he?' I interjected.

Holmes continued: 'His name is Harvey; he was leader of the London Saxophone Quartet, and respected in his profession, but like many saxophonists his search for the perfect mouthpiece became obsessive, until he craved to possess the mouthpiece of every player whom he admired. How he substituted one of his own mouthpieces for the Fabergé we may never know; probably he followed Beckenstein from Dover, and awaited his chance on the boat train.'

'But how did you know the substitute mouthpiece was his?' asked the American.

'Elementary, my dear Regni,' drawled Holmes, pulling his cape over his shoulders. 'The mouthpiece bore traces of what subsequent analysis proved to be black pudding; a revolting concoction consumed by Yorkshiremen, which Harvey was known to be. It also exuded a distinct odour of a particularly virulent variety of strong beer known as 'Gold Label'.'

(See my recent monograph on the recognition of three hundred and ninety seven brews of British beers). The most cursory inquiries of contacts in the music profession elicited the information that Harvey had lived on very little else but black pudding and Gold Label for years.

'But if my eyes do not deceive me, the fog is lifting, and we are just in time to catch the seven twenty three back to town. We will call at the Tavistock Hotel and deliver the Fabergé mouthpiece to its rightful owner. After that I must hurry to St James' Hall, as my friend Joachim has prevailed upon my good nature to deputise with his quartet on second violin, the man Ries being incapacitated from drink. I understand we are to be joined by a German clarinettist named Muhlfeld, to give the first British performance of a new Quintet by Herr Brahms.'

'After that perhaps you gentlemen would care to join me for a mouthful of lightly grilled steak at the Savoy . . . maybe with a little asparagus tossed in melted butter . . .'

The New York Saxophone Quartet on stage. l to r: Al Regni, Dave Tofani, Ray Beckenstein, Danny Bank.

Paul Harvey and Al Regni.

Al Regni, the alto player of the New York Saxophone Quartet, is a Sherlock Holmes nut. When they were in London once, I went round the shops with him looking for a deerstalker hat! So when Woodwind World wanted me to write a piece about them, rather than a dry recital of their respective biographies, I decided to enlist the help of Watson and Conan Doyle!

47

The study of the history of wind instrument design is not a discipline overburdened with light relief. I therefore make no excuse for the following saga which appeared in several consecutive issues of *Crescendo* in 1976. Neither am I ashamed of the fact that it was, partly, as I make Wally Horwood say in 'Unfair To Ophicleides', a publicity stunt for the World Saxophone Congress. Believe me, if you try to organize an event like that, you need all the publicity you can get, of which more later, in the chapter on the WSC.

THE 5th WORLD SAXOPHONE CONGRESS

When, in 1968, Paul Brodie first suggested the idea of a World Congress to help elevate the status of the saxophone, he could hardly have imagined how readily it would be taken up.

Under the sponsorship of Henri Selmer & Co. Ltd, the 1976 organisers are the London Saxophone Quartet — Paul Harvey, Hale Hambleton, Christopher Gradwell and David Lawrence — together with Stephen Trier. The Congress will be held at The Royal College of Music, close to the Royal Albert Hall in London, from Wednesday, July 28 to Saturday, July 31, 1976.

To announce the venture, a fine brochure has been prepared which outlines the aims of the London Congress and contains several excellent photographs and illustrations including one of the saxophone's inventor, Adolphe Sax. There is just one puzzle: What is a bass clarinet doing amid a cluster of saxophones of all sizes and many ages?

Paul Harvey writes to show how far the original aims have so far been realised, stressing the growth that has taken place through successive meetings in the number of participants, the number of specially written new works and the general worldwide interest in the instrument. The particular aim of the 1976 Congress is to attract more young players and to encourage more composers to write a first work for the saxophone. Reasons are given for the saxophone's neglect in the classical orchestra with a note of hope for the future in a revised instrumentation being favoured by contemporary composers.

As before, the Congress will feature concerts, recitals and master-classes with, I understand, a little more emphasis on the spoken word to relieve the ears after so much virtuoso playing. Particular stress is laid on the sociability aspect of the occasion and the value of exchanging thoughts and ideas with others outside of the concert hall.

Clearly, the 5th Congress is going to be something not to be missed, not only by saxophone addicts, but by all who value the true progressive spirit in music. Full particulars with Registration Forms are obtainable from The London Saxophone Quartet, 32 Maxwell Road, Welling, Kent DA16 2ES, England.

Bookings are expected to be heavy and accommodation in London at that time of year soon becomes full. Early appliction would therefore appear to be essential.

Wally Horwood

Crescendo **is proud to announce that our contributor Wally Horwood has been asked to deliver a lecture on Adolphe Sax during the 5th World Saxophone Congress.**

LETTER

I feel I should throw some light upon the puzzle that Wally Horwood mentions in his article on the 5th World Saxophone Congress (*Crescendo,* November). He asks: 'What is a bass clarinet doing amid a cluster of saxophones of all sizes and many ages?' I'm surprised that Wally, of all people, being Britain's leading authority on Adolphe Sax, did not realise the symbolic import of this juxtaposition. In fact, the idea arose from Wally's own book 'Adolphe Sax, His Life and Legacy', which tells us how Sax's years of work on the improvement of the bass clarinet led to his eventual concept of the saxophone, possibly by crossing one with an ophicleide.

I like to imagine Sax sitting in his hip bath, idly playing with his ophicleide. Suddenly he removes the brass mouthpiece and replaces it with a bass clarinet mouthpiece which happens to be lying in the soap dish. This is the sound he's been searching for. With a cry of 'Eureka', or whatever the French equivalent is, he leaps from his bath and runs, starkers, up and down Rue Myrha, playing 'Harlem Nocturne'. No doubt Wally's scholarly mind will recoil in horror at this over-sensationalised reconstruction of a process which probably took several years of patient experimentation, but I'm sure his colleague Jack Carter remembers it well.

Perhaps we should have included an ophicleide in the picture as well, but the point about the bass clarinet is that it hints at some of the saxophone's ancestry; a subject which we hope to cover in the exhibition of instruments being planned for the congress.

Paul Harvey

WALLY STRIKES BACK!

To have to explain a piece of symbolism is almost as bad as explaining a joke — it must fall flat! In the case of Paul Harvey's allegorical bass clarinet purporting to be the father of a clutch of saxophones, it deserves to. To suggest, as does this illustration, that the bass clarinet, as an instrument, played a major part in the development of the saxophone is, to my mind, misleading.

I have suggested — and it is only a suggestion — that Sax may have been trying to improve the notoriously unstable tones of the ophicleide and hit on the idea of removing the cup mouthpiece, substituting for it one with a single reed. Philip Bate and I carried out this experiment a few years ago using a bass clarinet mouthpiece taped to a rather ancient ophicleide. The resultant tone was significant.

To omit the ophicleide from the ancestry of the saxophone is to withold credit from the major progenitor. If we must liken the saxophone to other instruments, we might reasonably say that one of the larger sizes is an ophicleide with a single-reed mouthpiece. To assert that it is a wide conical-bored brass bass clarinet which overblows at the octave is clearly absurd. If the conjecture is correct, Sax took the mouthpiece from his bass clarinet, leaving the instrument itself lying silent and impotent in the corner. With this small piece of equipment, he coaxed the first saxophone-like tones from his amply-proportioned ophicleide.

If Adolphe Sax ever sat in a bath in the Rue Myhra, Paris, he must have been well past playing with his ophicleide or anything else. This was the street at No. 84, where Sax's sons carried on a modest business in the years immediately prior to the Second World War.

The bath-leaping episode, which those two benign pseudologists Paul and Jack are old enough to remember, might have occurred in the Rue de L'Evêque, Brussels. It was here that Charles Sax set up in business in the year of Waterloo and where possibly father and son worked together on saxophone prototypes during the 1830s.

Wally Horwood

UNFAIR TO OPHICLEIDES?

World Saxophone Congress is threatened

FROM OUR CRIME CORRESPONDENT

THERE were ugly scenes at the Annual General Meeting of the World Ophicleide Congress at the Memorial Hall, Boundstone, Surrey, last night.

AUDIENCE ENTHRALLED

A record audience, consisting of all six members, listened enthralled as Dr. Jack Carter (Professor of Benign Pseudology at the University of Charleston), delivered a witty lecture on "The Influence of Fluctuating Nodal Points on Ophicleide Multiphonics."

BRANDISHED CRESCENDO

Suddenly he was rudely interrupted as portly Yorkshireman Paul Harvey, wearing a cloth cap and black patent leather saxophone sling, burst into the hall brandishing a copy of last month's *Crescendo*.

ACCUSATIONS UNFOUNDED?

He flung the magazine into the face of the Chairman, influential local landowner and patron of the arts, Wally Horwood, shouting, "Your accusations of anti-Ophicleide discrimination are unfounded!"

PROVIDES OPHICLEIDE WORK?

He then produced a photograph of his popular group, "Musica di Camera di Bromley", which features an Ophicleide and a Keyed Bugle. "Here is proof that I provide work for needy Ophicleide players!" he screamed, flecks of foam dribbling down his chin. The police were called, and Harvey was ejected, singing "We Shall Overcome" in a cracked falsetto.

PUBLICITY STUNT?

Next morning, as Harvey was bound over to keep the peace, Mr. Horwood told Farnham Magistrates Court, "I suspect that the whole unseemly affair was a cheap publicity stunt for the World Saxophone Congress. Harvey and his creatures are worried about the competition from my World Ophicleide Congress. These benign pseudologists are all the same," he added with a throaty chuckle, "You have to watch them very carefully!"

Next month: An exclusive interview with Adolphe Sax.

Musica di Camera di Bromley, featuring Gunther Gradwell on Ophicleide.

OF COURSE, OF COURSE

It has been suggested by fellow-contributors P. Harvey and W. Horwood that I well remember the birth of Adolphe Sax's amusing little contribution to the family of musical instruments.

Of course, of course.

Actually, Adolphe didn't jump out of his bath shouting *Eureka!* — when the idea struck him. It's true he jumped out of his bath. So would anyone who sat on a carelessly dumped handful of screws and springs.

The idea struck him at breakfast. He was in the habit of summoning his family to the table by tootling on whatever instrument he was working on at the time. On this particular morning it happened to be a cylindrical object with a husky sound like a sheep suffering from tonsilitis.

'What on earth is that foul-looking, foul-sounding thing?' asked Mrs Sax.

Whereupon, to assert his authority, Adolphe struck the breakfast table a mighty blow with the cylindrical object and bent the end. As he was exceedingly frugal, and never threw anything away . . .

Jack Carter

AMAZING DISAPPEARANCE OF SAXOPHONE QUARTET
Shangri La tapes found

As you may have heard, the London Saxophone Quartet has disappeared in the Himalayas while on a British Council Tour of Tibet. The last anyone heard of them was the tape recording sent to the *Crescendo* office via the British Consulate in Kathmandu. It appears to have been recorded at an obscure monastery called Shangri La, and seems to be an interview with one of the residents by Paul Harvey. We have translated it, in case it is of interest to some readers . . .

Paul Harvey: 'Well, Monsieur Sax, first I must congratulate you upon your appearance, which, for a man of 162, is really amazing!'

Adolphe Sax: 'Pouf! mon fils, do yo sink zat I, who invented ze saxophone, would be defeated by such a simple problem as mortality?'

P.H.: 'But Wally Horwood, who is Britain's leading authority on you, is convinced that you died in 1894.'

A.S.: 'Zat is what I wanted people to sink ... all zose interminable lawsuits ... Mon Dieu! ... I 'ad 'ad enough! I bribed my doctor to procure a cadaver from his friendly neighbourhood body snatcher, and pass it off as me. Zen I made my way 'ere; an old monk 'ad told me of ze place. At last I found peace and contentment.'

P.H.: 'How do you pass your time?'

A.S.: 'I 've a little workshop in ze monastery cellar, mon brave. I 'ave made a complete set of quarter-tone saxophones, and am teaching ze monks to play zem for zeir Bhuddist ceremonies.'

P.H.: 'Fantastic ... but to return to your old life in Paris for a moment ... can you settle an argument? You see, there's this magazine called *Crescendo* ...'

A.S.: 'Zut alors! ... *Crescendo?* ... Of course I know zis journal; I read 'im every month. I 'ave ze standing order at W. H. Smith's in Lhasa. The benign M'sieu Carter ... ze informative M'sieu Evans ... ze omnipotent M'sieu Matthews ... even ze empirical M'sieu 'Orwood ... I feel zey are all old friends!'

P.H.: 'Well then, about this ophicleide and bass clarinet business, and how you invented the saxophone ...?'

A.S.: 'Ahhhh ... ze ohpicleide ... yes ... a noble instrument ... and ze bass clarinet too ... I love zem both like zey were my own children. But 'ow I invent ze saxophone ... zat's another kettle of herrings ... it's a long story ... are you sitting comfortably, mon gars? Zen I'll begin ...'

At this point the tape is broken. A note from the British Consul in Kathmandu explains that a portion of it was unfortunately eaten by a yak, during its hazardous transportation across the Himalayas. Fortunately the final part of the tape is intact.

P.H.: 'Well, M. Sax, I'm sure our readers will be most grateful to you for putting an end to that controversy once and for all! I'm only sorry that you won't be able to honour us by being guest of honour at the World Saxophone Congress, but we all understand the unfortunate effects of the outside world on residents of Shangri La. Finally, would you care to say a few words about your reaction to recent musical trends ... have you ever heard any jazz, for instance?'

A.S.: 'Like, I sought you'd never ask, homme! Yeah, we're really into Le Jazz Hot scene 'ere. Some of ze guys 'ave formed a really great rehearsal band. I'm lead alto, of course, and our arranger, Hec Berlioz, ' as done zese great charts ...'

P.H.: 'Did you say Berl ...?'

A.S.: '... with sort of a Kenton feel, but more kinda Shangri La, you dig? Hey ... howsabout finishing ze tape wiz a track from our latest LP? Zis one 'as some great solos ... like Joe Brahms on tenor, and some groovy ...'
P.H.: 'You don't mean Joha ...?'
A.S.: '... trombone work by Gus Mahler. As for ...'
P.H.: 'not *the* Mah ...?'
A.S.: '... Johnny Bach's trumpet ... yeah ... and real driving piano ...'
P.H.: 'B ... B ... B ... Ba ...?'
A.S.: '... from Frankie Liszt, and that drum break ...'
P.H.: Don't tell me ...'
A.S.: '... Yeah ... that ole "Mutt'n'Jeff Beethoven sure lays down a mean beat!'
P.H.: 'But everyone thinks they're d ...'
A.S.: 'So, 'ere we go, mes chats; ze Shangri La Big Band, wiz "Immortality Stomp".'

A limited number of copies of the performance which concludes the tape have been made and can be obtained from the Crescendo *office, price £753,000.00, plus V.A.T.*

Saul Tarvey

To think I always thought that Ophicleide was one of Shakespeare's more unfortunate heroines ... Ed.

POOF BREEDERS WANTED
CUSS NEWS GLASSERY
By Paul Harvey

(Paul Harvey *provides the following explanatory comments on how the article below came about:* 'I understand some members of the ICS are now receiving Cass News, *the journal of the British Clarinet & Saxophone Society. They may have been bewildered by some of the spelling in the last issue; I know we agree to differ on color/colour, quarter note/crotchet and all the rest, but, like, this is ridiculous, man! Those of a more mundane turn of mind may have thought it was due to a change of printer, or some such boring explanation. I therefore append this brief Glossary to show that we at* Cass *are into some really esoteric fields of research.' — Ed).*

The last issue contained references to several composers and works which may be unfamiliar to less well-informed readers. We therefore offer some further information which may be of interest to them and to musicologists in general.

(page 11) **Gerald Fuzi** (1901–1956). This British composer of Italian ancestry is perhaps best known for his song 'The Flat Foot Fuzi with the Floy Floy', as recorded in 1928 by the Electric Light Orchestra. His detractors have hinted that he was AC/DC, but such scandalous speculation is beyond the scope of our present assessment. His Clarinet Concerto was first performed by **Theo King** (p. 11); (Theodore Denner Klosé King, once Band Sergeant Major of the Royal Marines, Chatham Division) with a *Symphony* Orchestra conducted by **Rot Budden** (p. 16); a rather dry performance, according to some critics. (Apologies here to Thea King and Roy Budden, who were both friends of mine *ONCE!*)

(also p. 11 **Arnola Box** (1883–1953). Dame Ethel Smyth's most talented protegée, she gave up composition when she married Cuthbert Cox, a distinguished piano tuner. Together they started a thriving business for the production of Player-Piano Rolls. Using her full name, Petunia Arnola Box, they called the firm 'P. Arnola Box and Cox'.

(also p. 11, which is something of a collectors item): *Arthur Benjamin's* 'Tomscar de Ravel'. The title of this work refers to Ravel's cat; a rather vicious male. One day Ravel offered him 'Brand X' cat food instead of his favourite 'Moggynosh', and the brute marked him for life! Is it not ironic that this great master of orchestration should have missed out on his own cat?

(p. 12) **Kinsky-Korsckov** (1844–1908). There is much controversy over the rendering into English of Russian names. I suppose this is a viable alternative to the more usual Kinky-Coarsercough, and a definite improvement over the now little used Rippis-Korsetsoff.

(p. 14) **Francis Poulech** (1899–1963). Accused of being 'chicken' by the Maquis, this French composer escaped from France during the occupation and settled in Wales, where he made a name for himself with stirring nationalistic songs such as 'Hommes d'Harlech'.

Well, that's all I have time for now, as (p. 15) Barbara Wifflesworth and I are off to Tokyo in the morning to visit the Yamaha saxophone factory. I have achieved my life's work in this country, which has been to eradicate the dreaded spelling of saxophone as *SAXAPHONE*. In this, at least, I seem to have been successful!

4 Verse

I've always enjoyed writing verse of the doggerel variety, but most of it is unpublishable, being either in the form of scurrilous limericks or lovelorn Sonnets to ladies who are now respectable matrons with brawny sons who would challenge me to duels if I revealed their mothers' youthful indiscretions.

The Seven Deadly Virtues, however, should offend no one. It was commissioned for a Wigmore Hall concert which the soprano, Susan Roe, was to share with the LSQ and we needed a light-hearted Finale in which we could all participate. We also performed it with Meriel Dickinson at the LSQ's 10th Anniversary at St John's, Smith Square.

The Skiving Song was a sort of 'in joke' encore, to follow a performance of *The Seven Deadly Virtues* at Kneller Hall.

My daughter has been an opera buff from an early age, and there was a period when we used to write limericks on the backs of envelopes in the bar at the Coliseum. This is, perhaps, the best example of the genre:

THE MAGIC FLUTE

An elderly Queen of the Night
Gave Tamino a terrible fright.
When she hit her top F
He went totally deaf,
And the hair in his wig all turned white.

Lyrics from 'The Seven Deadly Virtues', an entertainment for Soprano (singer) and Saxophone Quartet.

HONESTY

(Chorus):
I'm as honest as the day is long
And I always speak as I find.
To be frank can never be wrong;
You have to be cruel to be kind!

Darling, what a lovely hat;
I'd love a hat like that;
But if I may speak both bold and true,
Don't you think it's a little too young for you?

(Chorus)

Darling, what a super trouser suit;
It's stylish and extremely cute.
I'm your honest friend who'd never snigger,
But you shouldn't wear trousers with your figure . . .

(Chorus)

Isn't this a super quartet?
Each one of them's a pet,
But I'll have to be honest and tell them soon
It's a pity they play so out of tune . . .

(Chorus)

VERSATILITY

Yes, I'd like to come to dinner one day,
Maybe after the opening of my current play;
I know I promised to come last week,
But the Oxford Union asked me to speak.
For our previous date I must beg pardon;
They did one of my Operas at Covent Garden
And last July I did my best,
But they needed my off spinners for the second test . . .
Just a minute, while I have a rest.

Well, now my novel's in the best seller list
I hope to make up for our dates I've missed,
But first I've got some recitals to do;
Violin, lieder and piano too.
If I seem preoccupied, don't be mad at me,
I have to paint a picture for the Royal Academy
And when I've finished that, my new venture starts;
A television series on the Martial Arts,
Cooking, sewing, ski-ing, rowing,
Handbell ringing, Highland flinging,
They're all my style,
I'm versa . . . (QUARTET: OH, SHUT UP!) . . . tile.

JOIE DE VIVRE
(Sung to an inversion of Offenbach's Can Can)
Early on a Monday morning, that's when I feel at my best,
Cracking jokes and laughing loudly in a way that's most endearing.
I don't care if others feel like something that the cat brought in;
I just go on laughing gaily, making a terrific din.

A dreary Monday morning's just the time to chuckle, just the
    time to laugh,
        (Ha, ha, ha, ha, ha, ha, ha)
Let other people grumble, jealous of my joie de vivre and
    a half!

THRIFT
I'm sorry I can't buy a round;
I'm saving up to buy a car.
Though pennies these days don't go far,
With thrift they soon become a pound.

I really can't buy you a drink;
I'm saving up to buy a house.
My meals would scarce sustain a mouse,
But listen to my pockets chink.

Now pay me back, and make it snappy;
I'm saving up to buy a yacht,
For everything I haven't got
Is what I need to make me happy.

I can't afford to send a letter;
I'm saving up to buy a plane.
I'll say my motto once again;
A penny's good, but a pound is better!

My airplane gracefully descends;
Its mighty engines roar like thunder,
But as I land I sometimes wonder
Why I haven't any friends!

DEMOCRACY

(Spoken)

Soprano (sax):
    Let's try that chord again;
    To say it goes against the grain,
    But I feel the tenor's rather flat.
Tenor:
    WHAT? No, no, no, it can't be that;
    The alto must be sharp.
Alto:
    Now just a minute; let's not harp
    On intonation so; it's my avowed
    Opinion that the baritone's too loud.
Baritone:
    It's generally agreed, by those who understand,
    My pianissimo is really rather grand.
    The trouble here is obviously aloft;
    I'd say that the soprano's much too soft.
Soprano:
    But I make sure my note can't be ignored,
    As it's the most important in the chord.
Alto, tenor and baritone, together:
    WHAT RUBBISH — the important note is MINE;
    My balance in the chord is fine!
Soprano (sax):
    Well, anyway, let's play the chord once more
    And try to put right what was wrong before.
Soprano (singer):
    If you don't mind a stranger butting in,
    I'd say your general sound is rather thin.
    The tenor's sharp, the alto's flat,
    The balance would be better if the baritone sat
    Where the soprano is . . .
Quartet:
    SHUT UP . . . MIND YOUR OWN BUSINESS!

ORIGINALITY
Once I wrote a piece where all the players banged their
　　instruments on the floor,
　　　　But that's been done before.
So then I wrote a piece where first they play a note, then sing,
　　　　But that's not really a new thing.
So then I wrote one where they don't play at all . . .
　　　　They just sit staring at the wall . . .
　　　　A pregnant silence fills the hall . . .
　　　　And yet this piece soon starts to pall . . .
　　　　It's not original at all!

But now I have discovered an original technique;
I've worked it out completely, and now's the time to speak.
The highest instrument plays a TUNE (yes, I know the very
　　thought of it makes you grit your teeth).
And the other three play CHORDS, which fit together
　　underneath!
　　　　So there you are; now THAT'S a different sound.
You've never heard the like before this, I'll be bound.
But the tragic outcome's what I most abhor;
Now that I've done it, it won't be original any more!

ERUDITION
I never use one syllable where four or five will do.
When contributing programme notes or writing a review.
My literary style is quite astonishingly new,
It's wonderful to know that I'm not ignorant like YOU!
　　　(The harmonic materials present an ascerbic combination of polytonal
　　　and chromatic techniques with powerful and punctuating clusters for
　　　maximum impact of acrid dissonance . . .)
I was a music student once, but soon I came to see,
That playing or composing were beneath the likes of me.
With dictionary poised I'm into musicology;
As long as no one understands it, I have earned my fee.
　　(plus VAT)
　　　(Electic impressionism is the matrix of this referential area inculcated
　　　as it is with macrotonic sequential development . . .)

Now here we have four samples of the ignorant musician,
Who merely plays his instrument and has no erudition.
I always like to have a few of these on exhibition,
To help you in assessing my superior position.
> (The retrograde inversion of the primary tone cell is here reversed to form an interstructural incursion into an inferior tessitura . . .)

But soon these types will disappear as if they'd never been,
As my new kind of concert takes its place upon the scene;
No musical distractions for the audience between
My eruditest programme notes projected on a screen!
> (The constructivist elements of the form-plan development such as fragmented clusters non-referential isolation and electronic mutations create a dialectic of formal organization highlighting the disparity of levels between these two strata at the same time avoiding the complete serialisation of all parameters while emphasising the dodecaphonic interplay and aleatoric melismas which are essential to the juxtaposition of its interdependent tonal centres . . .)

MODESTY

And so our final virtue then is modesty,
As exemplified by the composer of this oddity.
He tells me his ambition,
Which now has reached fruition,
Is to make his composition
As bad as his poetry.

Yes a third rate composer is what he wants to be,
And I think he has achieved it, with this you must agree,
But how can we criticize him when he's done his best
To write a piece which even he must heartily detest.

Well I've known some mad composers,
But this one beats the lot;
A great poet and composer
He certainly is not,
Yet because of some strange twisted exhibitionism he
Displays the fact in public with a masochistic glee.

He steals tunes from great composers just to get an easy laugh . . .
Why he does it I can't tell you, it must be some strange compulsion
From the depths of his unconscious, now he can't think how to finish,
But I bet he'll soon be starting on his final stupid tune . . .
And he's even given up trying to rhyme the words . . .

THE SKIVING SONG

This is a little ditty to be sung to the tune of the Kneller Hall School March, which is 'Blow Away the Morning Dew'. Here is the slightly 'martialised' version of the tune, which all KH pupils know and love:

I also append a glossary for Americans and readers who haven't been in the army:

To skive .... to avoid work
The rock .... the outdoor bandstand at Kneller Hall
Booze .... alcoholic beverages
Birds .... young persons of the female gender
Dims and doms .... diminished seventh and dominant seventh arpeggios
Professors' Rolls .... the office where lesson times are allocated
Scrubout .... Scrubbing floors and cleaning barrack rooms
R.S.M. .... Regimental Sergeant Major
M.I. Room .... Medical Inspection Room
NAAFI .... Navy, Army and Air Force Institute
B.S.M. .... Band Sergeant Major (at KH, the senior Student Bandmaster)
Adjutant .... the officer in charge of discipline
Commandant .... the senior officer of the School
R.T.U. ....Return to Unit (KH equivalent of expulsion)

I never work if I can help it, I much prefer to skive,
I have a sore lip every day from eight o'clock till five,
'Cos with practising and all that stuff, I'm not enthused,

I skive away the morning dew, from blowing I'm excused.
When full band is playing on the rock, and everyone is hot and tired,
You can find me bedded down inside the block, my symptoms they are much admired.
But when the bugle blows at five my symptoms fade away,
Miraculous recovery's the order of the day
And I'm out among the booze and birds, Right on, Sport,
I skive away till morning dew and hope I don't get caught.

Now Mister Harvey's dims and doms, they really turn me off,
If I can't play them you should hear the way he'll sneer and scoff,
Yes he's really most unkind to me, what shall I do?
I'll telephone Professors Rolls and say I've got the 'flu.
Then I'll lie in bed and listen to the band rehearsing 'Caliph of Baghdad',
And I'll doze off soon and wake up feeling grand; I need my sleep 'cos I'm a growing lad.
My company commander later drops in for a chat,
It's scrubout evening in our block and I don't fancy that,
So I tell him I am feeling ill; I'm off my grub,
To see the doctor I go out but don't get past the pub.

The R.S.M. invited me to go out on parade,
'Oh sir,' I said 'I'd love to come, but I am so afraid
That my feet are killing me today, marchings to blame
From wearing boots I am excused, it really is a shame.'
In my bedroom slippers see me limp along, from M.I. room to NAAFI bar,
You can see how all that stamping would be wrong, I really couldn't march very far.
But in the evening I can squeeze my feet into my shoes,
Then I'll parade up Whitton High Street after birds and booze
But you'll never see me on parade out on the square,
I'll skive away the morning dew, for that I've got a flair.

The B.S.M. he had me charged, I just can't tell you why.
The Adjutant to understand me didn't even try,
So I went before the Commandant, my case was reviewed,
It didn't do me any good, I've just been R.T.U.'d.
So it's back to my Batallion I must go, rejected now and in disgrace,

But I'll soon be back to my old tricks, you know, still skiving in a different place.
So all you K.H. pupils better listen to my song,
And see if you can profit by the things that I did wrong,
Though you win the smartest pupil prize and do very well,
I'll bid you, with a smart salute, a skiver's fond farewell.

5 Uncle Paul's Problems

This is the point at which it must be clearly stated that this book in no way pretends to be a tutor. The complete 'Uncle Paul's Problem Page' saga from eleven early issues of *Cass News* (the journal of the Clarinet and Saxophone Society of Great Britain) is included because it illustrates my lifelong efforts to imbue these incredibly specialised topics with some leavening of humour.

Training the Little Fingers for their Big Job is interesting for being the first article I ever sent off to the USA. I remember reading an early issue of *Woodwind World* in the Central Music Library and thinking, 'Why shouldn't I write something like this?'

UNCLE PAUL'S PROBLEM PAGE

The Editorial Committee of CASS suspects that some beginners on clarinet or saxophone may be overawed by the exceedingly esoteric erudition of our journal. Therefore they have delegated me, as the most simple-minded member of the committee, to write a series of articles for beginners, couched in the most straightforward, nitty-gritty-plumbing terms possible. So welcome to 'Uncle Paul's Problem Page'. I hope you will write in with interesting problems and queries, but meanwhile I must start the ball rolling by posing a couple of the commonest myself.

A favourite pre-beginner question is: 'Is it better to start on the clarinet or the saxophone?' Now I don't mind coming right out and saying it's best to start on the clarinet, for the following reasons: a beginner on clarinet will start in the bottom register, therefore getting to know the several leger lines below the treble stave right from the start, and when he advances into the upper register will become used to the two different twelfth apart fingerings. On changing to saxophone, the two registers being an octave apart and having basically the same fingering will seem simpler. Also it's best for the beginner's fingers to learn to cope with covering the clarinet's open holes first, before experiencing the greater freedom of position allowed by the saxophone finger plates.

However, do not imagine for a moment that I'm saying the saxophone is easier to play. It only seems to be to a clarinettist for about the first five minutes. Stand by for Great Thought No. 1: THE SAXOPHONE IS A VERY EASY INSTRUMENT TO PLAY BADLY.

Many beginners have been told to blow from their diaphragm, but are confused as to how this is actually achieved. The simplest way to explain it is that blowing out a candle, 'PHEW' is wrong. 'HUH', as for streaming up a mirror ready to polish it is right. Hold your hand in front of your mouth and go 'PHEW'; your breath feels cold; that's wrong. Go 'HUH' onto your hand and your breath will feel warm; that's the stuff to pump into your clarinet. Stand with your back to a wall and press the back of your head against it. Remove the belt from your trousers (or skirt) so that you have to hold them up with your stomach muscles. Blow long notes on your clarinet, and making sure your trousers don't finish up around your ankles will ensure diaphragmatic blowing.

This technique will be useful later in your career if both your belt and braces (I always wear both with evening dress as I'm a worrier) let you down during a recital.

So don't forget to write in with those problems; in future issues I may discuss such burning issues as tonguing, causes of squeaks, does playing the basset horn cause dandruff, or any other topic which you care to ask about.

Dear Mr Harvey,

As a member of CASS, I always read your articles with interest and enjoyment. I notice in the latest issue you ask for queries about playing problems. I wonder if you might be able to help me with one of mine?

This concerns trouble with low notes – C, B and B flat – on alto saxophone. After playing for a time, I find security on these notes increasingly difficult, almost as if the embouchure refused to relax. Changing around mouthpieces and reeds makes no difference. I use a Selmer 'Soloist' F facing and 2½ grade Rico Royal reeds. This combination gives good control and tone over the rest of the range.

Ian P. C. Robertson

ANSWER:

This of course is the eternal problem of the saxophone: how to play the bottom notes softly, which is common to all conical bore woodwind instruments. The first thing that strikes me in your letter is that an F mouthpiece is much too open for any style of playing except the hairyest jazz. I use a B lay on soprano and a C on alto, mainly because I could not control the bottom notes on anything wider.

Secondly, check that all your pads are covering well, as the tiniest leak, which does not affect the rest of the range, will cause bubbling on low notes.

The rest is a matter of practice. Here is a very good way to improve your low notes. Try to play down a bottom octave scale with your octave key OPEN. You will find that you have to increase your wind pressure enormously, and will probably peter out below G at first. It's best to do this out of earshot of anyone else, as it sounds like a sick cow. However, if you persevere, when you go back to playing with the octave key closed, the bottom register seems much easier by comparison.

Also try to develop sub-tone low notes; my way is to slide the top teeth towards the tip of the mouthpiece and push the bottom lip out to cover as much reed as possible. INCREASE wind pressure AND lip pressure; this seeming contradiction stifles the reed's vibration and results in a more unobtrusive sound. I also let an air pocket under my top lip. This sub-tone is frowned upon by the purest of serious saxophonists in France, as is the dreaded 'doughnut' or saxophone mute, which can be inserted into the bell. However, I make no secret of the fact that I always have a doughnut ready for symphony orchestra dates, where one's reputation usually depends on being able to play low notes softly. It is easily constructed from a roll of cloth or one of those doughnut shaped things ladies use for their hair. My own is a piece of old shirt wound around with string. It is most effective in taming notes down to C, and for bottom B turn it sideways in the bell. If you get a pianissimo bottom B flat, play it on the tenor, or send a dep!

Three orchestral solos for which I consider a doughnut invaluable can be found in Vol. 1 of Chester's new publication, *Saxophone Solos*. These are *L'Arlesienne* by Bizet, *Harry Janos* by Kodaly, and *Sylvia* by Delibes.

In this issue I do not offer a solution to a problem, rather an exhortation to face up to, and make the best of one. (I'll never make *Woman's Own* at this rate!) I've had a spate of letters recently on the lines of: 'My Daddy has just bought me a Buffmer and Yamahawkes solid gold soprano saxophone with platinum keys and mink lined pads. Although it cost a lot of money, it sounds all out of tune. Can you tell me where I can get a soprano which is perfectly in tune?'

As a youth I had it dinned into me by my teacher never to discuss Politics, Religion or Intonation, but the time has come to speak out on the last subject. It has to be faced that there is no such thing as a 'perfectly in tune' instrument of any kind. Our task in selecting an instrument is to be able to recognize the least out of tune one.

Imagine we are testing a new clarinet. First blow a middle line B against an A tuning fork. It's best if this is 'bright' (euphemism for sharp) rather than 'dull' (euphemism for flat) as you then have some leeway to pull out, but if your clarinet is flat there is nothing you can do, except get a shorter barrel. The most critical notes on the clarinet are the 'throat notes', that is G, A flat, A and B flat between 2nd and 3rd lines. Test these by playing major chords from an octave below: i.e., A, C sharp, E, A, etc. If the barrel is pushed in, these should be bright, so you can flatten them by putting your right hand down. As you pull out, the throat notes are affected more than the rest of the instrument, so if they're dead in tune to begin with, they'll be flat when pulled out, and that's trouble!

The upper register of the clarinet is one big compromise. Ted Planas says the only way to get it in tune would be for every note to have its own speaker hole; imagine the mechanical complexity of that! (I expect Ted's working on it). The top register differs between each individual instrument. Test each note again by major chords from an octave below. Don't forget flatness at the top is usually caused by lack of wind pressure from the diaphragm, or the wrong 'oral cavity'. The difference between thinking 'EEEEEEE' and 'ORRR' can be as much as a minor third.

For more detailed insight into how experienced players make the best of these problems see Jack Brymer's recent book on the clarinet, especially pages 75–89, and you'll soon realize that the basic fingering chart in your tutor hardly scratches the surface.

As regards the saxophone, the instrument is a victim of its own flexibility; it has to be approached like singing or playing the violin. A general rule, especially for the soprano, is to tune it bright and blow it down to pitch, as this results in a warmer sound than if you're squeezing up. There is a grain of truth in the old adage. 'It's better to play sharp than out of tune.'

I have had so many heart-rending cries for help lately from frustrated soprano enthusiasts that I intend to hold some soprano clinics at the Woodwind Workshop in August to reveal some fascinating developments in the improvement of this hitherto neglected instrument. The subject is so involved I can't begin to compress it into the space of this article: we can only approach it through demonstration and experimenting together. At the moment there are more soprano saxophones than people in my house, and the cat has had a nervous breakdown. But we must soldier on with our pioneering work, keeping as our watchwords: 'Experiment, Flexibility and Compromise'.

I've had two enquiries about top notes: one each for clarinet and saxophone. I'll start with the clarinet, as it is easier to produce harmonics on the cylindrical bore. Cyril Pepper writes:

I'm still having difficulty with the upper register, especially the top three notes. Apart from stretching the lower lip, what other tips can you give me (other than take up plumbing!) to produce a clear full tone? I would greatly appreciate any hints.

The best way to approach the top register of the clarinet is to erase completely from your mind any consideration of lip or embouchure. Concentrate on the inside of your mouth and your diaphragm. Play octaves up to the top register, thinking 'ORRR up an octave EEEEEE' with a crescendo which seems to come from your toenails (via your diaphragm, of course). If the top note is flat, try doing a glissando downwards and sliding back up to the note (EEORREEEE). After a bit you'll find that you've slid up to a higher pitch than before. Any of my pupils who mention embouchures, or utter the dreaded obscenity 'lipping it up', have to write out one hundred times: 'I have no embouchure; just a hole in my face, which is the outward and visible manifestation of my diaphragm, whence cometh tone, high notes and all manner of good things.'

As regards the top three notes: B flat is a harmonic of long F, but it wants to be a G. It is your job to persuade it otherwise. Try this exercise:

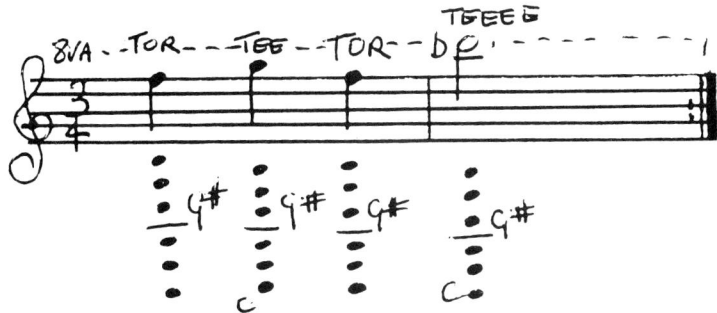

B is a harmonic of long F sharp, and can be helped by the first finger left hand opening the G sharp key (keeping its hole covered at the same time).

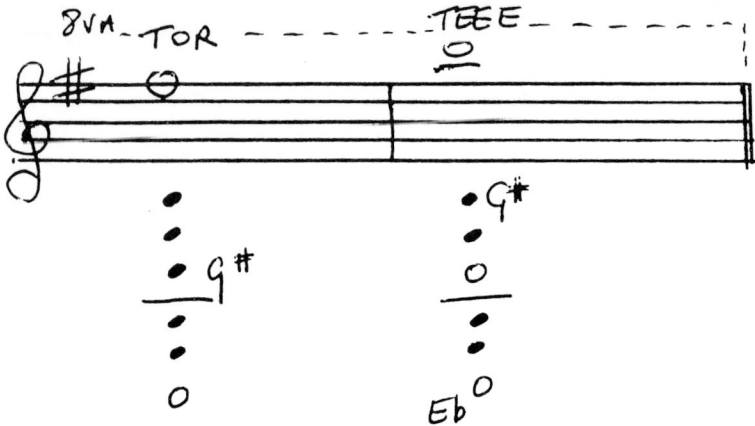

C is a harmonic of G, and is similarly helped by the first finger left hand opening the A key.

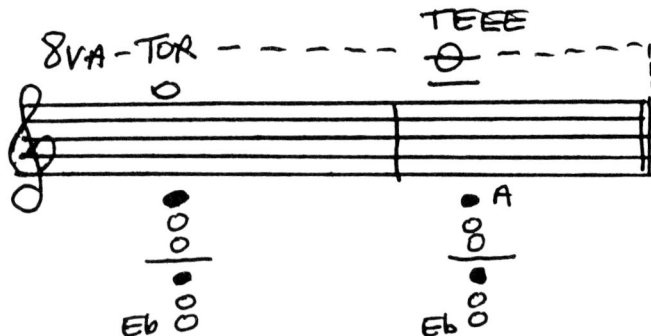

Mind you, Cyril, to paraphrase Jules Feiffer, 'I always wanted to be a plumber, but instead I have to sit playing the clarinet all day just to make a living. The world should make a place for plumbers!' (Have you tried to get one lately?)

So, from plumbing it's an easy step to the saxophone. Wally Horwood writes:

Your tip in the last CASS News about the doughnut has worked wonders with a Karl Meyer tenor I have acquired and which, I am told, is notorious for not producing its bottom notes at all, let alone softly. Could you now give us some tips about the other end of the register – how to approach the harmonics for those who have never attempted them before? Uncle Paul's beginner's guide to the altissimo register would be much appreciated.'

Step One: Buy *Eugene Rousseau's Saxophone High Tones (Etoile).*

Step Two: Practise the natural overtones before attempting any high notes.

Step Three: Remember, Great Uncle Ted says that the nodal pressure point for the saxophone is much further down your throat than for the clarinet, so imagine you're a Yorkshire born soprano (singer, not saxophone) singing the Queen of the Night's aria standing on a chair with mice running underneath; go EEEEEE and blow like 'ell. After playing top C on the soprano I feel as if I've received a karate chop in the adam's apple.

Step Four: Don't take any altissimo fingering charts too literally (especially mine); every saxophone I've every played has had different harmonic fingerings. The most awkward to pitch are G and G sharp; it may be easier to start with A to C and come back later to the gap. Just to prove what a benevolent old Uncle I am, here, free of charge, are my current altissimo fingerings for soprano:

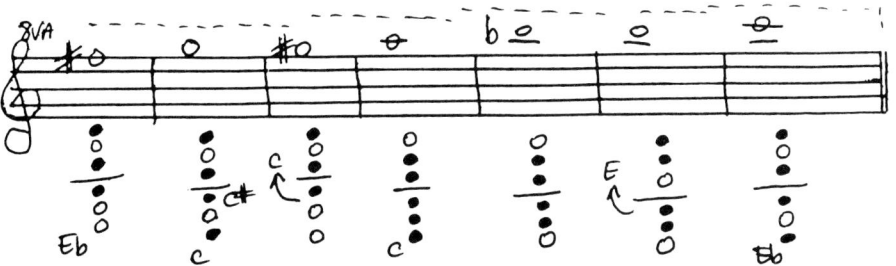

and the best of luck, mate!

I've decided to write about some of my own pupils' problems this time. Having recently started the new course at Kneller Hall, I've surveyed my twenty or so new clarinet pupils, and have listed all their problems, in order of popularity. Top of the charts is undoubtedly insufficient wind going into the instrument. The cause of this may be psychological (if I blow too hard I might squeak, causing this fierce looking clarinet professor to fly into an ungovernable rage at my incompetence') or physical; insufficient diaphragm support or not enough mouthpiece in the mouth. The latter is by far the most popular embouchure problem. If the lower lip is clamped like a vice on the tip of the reed, there's hardly any gap for the wind to get through, however hard you blow. Putting more mouthpiece in gives you a bigger sound and makes high notes easier to get. If you go too far you'll be liable to squeak a lot, so you have to experiment to find the most you can get into your mouth without becoming a bad squeak risk. I find that Vandoren mouthpieces work better if you take a little more into your mouth than you would with other makes.

Next come the various bad postures and instrument positions when playing sitting down. There's really only one way to play the clarinet properly; that is with the bottom right at the back of the chair, trunk erect, head upright, clarinet at 45 degrees to the body, bell just over the space between your knees. Any deviation from this position should be corrected before getting any worse. Bad positions and corrective techniques are as follows:

    Head down, bell up. Put music stand as high as possible and tie piece of string from bell to pupil's foot.

    Head up, bell down. Put music stand as low as possible and tie string from bell to some fixture over pupil's head (or to the music stand).

    Bell to right or left. Tie bell to the opposite knee.

In all these corrective positions you must make sure the pupil's head does not just follow the instrument, thereby retaining the same faulty relative position.

With regard to hand position, the thumbs are often overlooked. When playing open G, G sharp or A, pupils' left thumbs often jump down on the wood of the upper joint below the thumb hole, instead of hovering over the hole and speaker key, ready for instant action. To correct this a large lump of cork can be sellotaped to the upper joint just below the thumb hole, making this involuntary thumb twitch impossible.

Almost without exception my current crop of pupils had the thumb rest too far towards the base of their right thumb. Having it almost level with the thumbnail improves the right technique spectacularly. Another lump of cork sellotaped to the left of the thumbrest will prevent the thumb going too far across.

The quality of tonguing is very good this year, and I have almost no huffers, grunters, oinkers or jellybellies. (See my Monograph *A Definitive Treatise On Pathological Deviations from Correct Clarinet Tonguing Techniques*, soon to be serialised in *News of the World*).

I leave you with a sobering thought. (Not that you habitually read my column in a state of intoxication, I trust!) None of the pupils were aware that they had these problems; they all thought there was something wrong with their mouthpiece, reed or instrument!

First we have a question about the logistics of saxophone playing. 'Can you give your opinion on whether the alto saxophone should be played between the legs or outside the right leg when sitting down. Also do you favour a stand or sling for the baritone?'

This has always been a bone of contention; the tenor is obviously built on a slant, and can only be played outside the right leg, but both positions are possible for the alto. For many years I played on an old Conn alto, between my legs, and maintained uncompromisingly that this was the correct position. Then I sold the Conn to a pupil and bought a Selmer Mk. 6. I was preparing for the first performance of Gordon Jacob's *Miscellanies,* so was doing more alto practice than usual. To my horror I found I was chewing up my bottom lip, after years of scornful scoffing at pupils who complained of sore lips. 'Ho, ho, foolish lad, *I* never get a sore lip, because I don't pull too much over my bottom teeth, and I do everything with diaphragm pressure, etc., etc., . . . blah . . . blah'. How the lads laughed as they saw me spitting blood and desperately moulding misshapen gutta percha teeth shields!

Then the pupil who'd bought my old Conn came for a lesson. When I saw the two altos together I realised that the crook of the Selmer bent at a narrower angle than the Conn. By playing it between my legs I had been allowing the reed to push my bottom lip onto my teeth. As soon as I moved it outside my right leg, the angle of the mouthpiece sloped down more, and the pressure on my lip was relieved! So now I say; keep an open mind, and experiment to find which position is best for the shape of YOUR alto, because the crook angle of different makes varies much more than you might think.

What baritone playing I have done has usually been in a doubling situation, where a ball and socket type stand is essential. Most baritone specialists, however, such as David Lawrence and all top quartet baritone players, prefer a sling because it gives them more control of top notes; on a stand the instrument tends to fall away from you when you open the top keys.

From a young clarinettist, another question about the top-register: 'Which fingerings do you prefer for top G, as all the fingering charts I have seen give different ones?'

You could write a book about top G on the clarinet, though I doubt if any publisher would accept a book on so specialised a subject! My favourite general purpose G is:

which is the one given by Klose, who, after all, did invent the Boehm system. E flat all with thumb & speaker key on

If I have to leap up to a staccato G,
and want to avoid it sounding flat, I use:

which is generally bright enough
without the right little finger
E flat key open.

B flat side key

Very useful for F sharp-G trills and fast G major scales is:
but don't stay on that one, as it's usually flat.

The harmonic of B is useful in certain runs, such as in
the 3rd movement of the Malcolm Arnold Sonatina, but
again, I find it rather flat to dwell upon.

A lesser known one is:
which happens to be the
best G on my E flat clarinet,
and is a handy fingering for the
C-G leaps in the Rossini
Variations. So its all a matter of your individual instrument and the sort of passage in which the G appears. There are lots of other fingerings, so why not experiment a bit, and make up your own list with the possible uses and characteristics of each one?

Uncle Paul is really in trouble this time! He's had a letter from a lady clarinettist in Switzerland, asking 'What effect does pregnancy have on clarinet playing?' and signed 'Your Obedient Niece'. It's difficult to imagine a question more outside my experience, as I have never had a pupil at Kneller Hall in this 'interesting condition'; the modern Army is certainly more liberral than in my soldiering days, but there ARE limits! I could make a glib reply suggesting that the situation could be avoided altogether by assiduous study of Jean-Marie Londeix's *Rhythm Method* but, although I make no claim to omniscience I do pride myself on being able to find out almost anything by picking other people's brains. I have therefore sought the advice of several lady clarinettists who double as wives and mothers, sidling furtively up to them in the RCM canteen or at CASS meetings, asking them intimate questions in a hoarse whisper. Those who did not slap my face or set their husbands on me have provided the following information!

If the baby is 'lying low' it's OK to continue playing, but if it's 'lying high' you should stop for the last 4–6 weeks. (I don't understand that either, but it sounds nice and scientific). Playing standing is more difficult than sitting, as body-balance is changed, and backache a problem; good posture is therefore most important. One lady I interviewed said she had actually played the contrabasss clarinet during pregnancy, but didn't advise it, as she felt 'as if she was about to give birth on the spot'! (One way to get clarinet choirs in the news, I suppose). I think Doctor members of CASS should write in and continue this topic, as I'm feeling most inadequate. Therefore, removing my white coat and stethoscope, I will pass on to the next query, from the same lady in Switzerland.

She has a pupil who cannot bend the ring finger of his left hand, owing to actual physical lack of a joint, which causes squeaks. I think the only solution when it is not physically possible to cover any open hole due to a deformity or injury to a finger is to have a plate fitted over that hole, making it a covered hole. There have been cases of players who have lost the top joint of a finger having a plate fitted which extends out to meet the shorter finger. My correspondent mentions a Swiss colleague who is a skilled instrument mechanic, so he should be interested in the problem. One sometimes comes across old covered hole clarinets, from which a plate can be taken to save making one.

She also asks what to do about some 'great big laddies' whose symptoms of puberty include unwillingness to practise, lack of tone, musicianship and general *joie de vivre*. I might suggest easy jazz duets or writing out pop tunes in block harmonies, but I expect she's tried that sort of thing. No, she obviously expects an answer with a bit of *je ne sais quoi*. How about this? Introduce them to an equal number of nubile girl pupils, and set up a research project to answer her first question. This should be a dead cert for a research grant from her local University, and I look forward to receiving my complimentary copy of her Doctoral Thesis in nine months' time.

After the last issue's voyage into the hazardous waters of obstetrics, it is a relief to set foot on dry land once more with a couple of questions on my favourite subject: fingerings. I know that the hand that rocks the cradle rules the world, but the hand that knows the right fingerings is also pretty important in the CASS world!

A saxophonist writes: 'Which is the best fingering of B flat? I always use button B flat, but have seen other players using the side key.' As with all alternative fingerings, the best one is that which suits the passage being played at the time. Button B flat (1st finger LH depressing button as well as B plate) is very useful for passages based on the chords of E flat major and G minor, or any rapid movement involving G–B flat. Its use is similar to the E flat/B flat spatula which you sometimes find on pre-war 10-10 clarinets. I have always noticed that people who start on the saxophone seem to use button B flat too much, while those who started on clarinet (like me) tend not to use it enough.

I consider the RH side key to be the most useful fingering, and use it in all scalic passages containing one flat or more, and chromatics. In fact it would be true to say that nearly all pages containing B flat are *possible* using the side key, whereas, although other fingerings may be better for some passages, there are many where they would be an encumbrance to smooth technique. My C soprano, in common with many old saxophones, has only side key B flat; no button, no RH linkage. So this must prove that side key B flat was originally the basic fingering.

My correspondent does not mention long B flat, which should not be overlooked, as there are three long fingerings on saxophone. 1st finger LH in combination with either 1st, 2nd or 3rd finger RH, all work equally well, with very slight variations of pitch which are often useful for fine intonation adjustments. Long B flat with first finger RH for chords of B flat, long B flat with middle finger RH for the chords of G flat/F sharp major or E flat minor. Besides these five conventional fingerings, there are various harmonic B flats, such as the fourth partial with all the holes on the instrument closed, but these are mainly useful as a practice technique and are rarely used in performance.

Now to a similar question about the clarinet. At the recent Woodwind Workshop I was taking a class on the chromatic scale, and the old discussion came up about RH side key versus LH 3rd finger 'top' key for E flat/B flat in chromatic passages. Many clarinet teachers prefer the top key, so as to keep the action on the same hand; indeed my old RCM professor, Ralph Clarke, was very keen on the top key, consequently I have always felt vaguely guilty about being able to play chromatics faster with the side key. So I decided to hold a mini referendum on the spot. Out of the twenty people present, twelve used the side key, seven the top key and one used top going up and side coming down! Maybe this proves something, maybe not; anyway, as far as I could ascertain, none of the ladies present was pregnant!

A member writes: *I am an amateur clarinettist with little time to spare for practice; can you suggest the best way to spend that time, and do you consider long note practice to be as essential as many people say?*

Long note practice is certainly very valuable; as a youth I spent many hours at this, with television turned on during test matches with the sound off. This is why I put in my biographical notes that I studied under Frederick Thurston, Len Hutton and Denis Compton. However, I have noticed a tendency in some assiduous practisers of long notes to play their daily dose of long notes with a fine sonorous tone, swelling to magnificent crescendo and fading away to a finely controlled pianissimo, well supported from the diaphragm, finely judged oral cavity for the pitch, and all the rest of it. Then they play a scale or exercise, and all this beautiful sound control disappears, because they are only thinking of their finger technique, having psyched themselves into equating sound production only with long notes. So my advice is to approach everything you play as a long note, especially scales and arpeggios. Play them slowly enough so that you can gauge the evenness of the transition from note to note in the steps of the scales and the bigger intervals of the arpeggios. As to the rest of your practice, if time is limited, and whose isn't; don't fritter it away waffling through things you can play already, really try to pick out some passages which you can't play, and flog them to death. The really difficult finger movements on the clarinet can be broken down into a remarkably small number of passages; movements such as E to B flat with the left hand around the throat notes.

My U.P.'s.P.P. file is bursting with letters from young members who are engaged in writing projects on the saxophone. It is very encouraging to see this, but unfortunately the saxophone lacks easily accessible sources of reference such as the clarinet enjoys in the Rendall, Weston, Brymer, etc. books. So I thought it might be helpful to list the sources I suggest to them. For information on Saxophone repertoire I recommend Jean-Marie Londeix *125 Years of Music for Saxophone* published by Leduc, available here from United Music Publishers or June Emerson. For history try *Adolphe Sax 1814-1894 — His Life and Legacy* by Wally Horwood (Egon Publishers).

The problem page is a rather offbeat one, owing to a couple of points which have arisen from Pamela Weston's review, in the last issue, described by one of my foreign correspondents as 'Your CLARINETTIST'S BEDBOOK' (sic). I hope ardent seekers after fingerings and exercises for the diaphragm will be patient meanwhile.

The first question comes from Manchester, saying: 'I was

interested that Pamela Weston mentions the use of metal clarinets at Kneller Hall. I am writing a thesis on the Instrumentation of Wind Bands, in which I have stated that metal clarinets have been virtually obsolete since the 1930s. Was I wrong? If so, what kind of metal clarinets are in use at Kneller Hall?'

No, you were not wrong. The only metal clarinets (apart from those in the museum) in use at Kneller Hall are Leblanc contrabasses. As you correctly stated in your thesis, metal were last used in army bands in the 1930s, and then mostly in India.

Another letter from a gentleman describing himself as 'Professor of Basset Horn at Tidworth College of Technology'. He writes, almost illegibly: 'Has the Franz Schaik, mentioned by Pamela Weston on p. 18 of the last *Cass News* any connection with Franz Schalk, composer of a Grand Fantasia on Rossini's *La Gazza Ladra*, or *The Silken Ladder?*'

Yes, indeed, the great Franz Schalk did adopt the nom de plume of Schaik on a couple of occasions. Once when he published a chart of trill fingerings for basset horn, and again on his return from a tour of the Middle East, when he advertised himself as 'Schaik of Araby'. He had no connection, however, with the contemporary Schaik who recently formed a trio with a well known conductor and pianist. (Would you believe Rattle and Roll?)

It is not generally known that Schalk spent the twilight of his years in England, in a modest villa in Neasden. He died there, forgotten, in 1880, a victim of terminal dandruff, the perennial scourge of basset horn players.

GOVERNMENT TRUTH WARNING . . . THIS INFORMATION IS FICTITIOUS, AND COULD BE INJURIOUS TO YOUR CREDIBILITY (and I bet you believed every word of it, too!)

By the way, correspondent of Tidworth, you may accuse me of nit picking (well, everyone must have some hobby) but you have confused *La Gazza Ladra (The Thieving Magpie)* with *La Scala di Seta (The Silken Ladder)*. A common mistake; indeed I seem to remember seeing it quite recently in a book of clarinet studies, but no doubt it has by now been rectified in subsequent editions.

The Editor has asked me to discourse upon slap tonguing. This was much overdone in the 1920s, but could be of use in contemporary music as a grotesque effect. Where slap tongue is sometimes called for in the French repertoire, such as in the cadenza of the Ibert *Concertino,* or the last movement of the Francaix *Quartet,* it is generally not performed with the full slap technique, as I am about to describe, but merely with a rather harder than normal attack.

The usual analysis of slap tongue is as follows: Place tongue flat against reed. Contract tongue muscles so that a vacuum forms between tongue and reed. Lower tongue, vacuum drawing reed down with it. Blow as reed springs back, slapping lay of mouthpiece.

This technique works best on larger reeds. Peter Ripper and I have recently developed an interesting alternative for alto and soprano in Pierre-Max Dubois' *Dessins Animés,* which is such a brilliant piece of writing we wanted to give it the full theatrical effect. For the alto slaps Peter opens his mouth wide at the same time as his attack, and I pull the soprano mouthpiece right out of my mouth as I tongue. Fortunately, only isolated slaps are called for, although, if we were able to perform fast runs like this, the visual impact would be pretty spectacular! Final word of warning: only experiment with slap tonguing if your legitimate tonguing technique is firmly established.

Now another query from Catherine Shrubshall, who is in the running for Uncle Paul's 'Miss Problem Page of 1981' award. She writes, 'Since starting at Trent Park College in Enfield, I have had reed problems. Back home in Thorpe-Le-Soken, reeds generally worked straight away, but here the ends go all crinkly and take quite a bit of licking and blowing before they work. Also my clarinet bell has split; is there a connection?

Yes, there is, because the whole problem is one of humidity, or rather, lack of it. This is a subject discussed much more by players in the USA, owing to their greater variations of altitude and climate. Thorpe-Le-Soken is almost at sea level, I imagine, in a pretty moist part of Essex. Enfield is a fair bit higher, and I seem to remember from a previous visit to Trent Park College, that the central heating is pretty fierce. This is the main factor, as central heating dries the atmosphere. If I was a better business man I would get you to send a postal order for 'Uncle Paul's Patent Humidifier' which would consist of a piece of orange peel in a plastic bag. Don't leave your reed on the mouthpiece overnight; put it in a reedguard to keep the tip flat, in the plastic bag with the orange peel. If you have to keep your instruments (especially clarinets) at college, put a saucer of water or a damp sponge in the locker with them. Thirsty mice will be very grateful.

WORSLEY, MANCHESTER
3 February

Sir,
I recently heard a broadcast performance by the BBC Northern Ireland Orchestra, of a suite of incidental music to *L'Arlesienne* by Bizet, in which passages written by the composer for alto saxophone were played in one instance by a horn and in another by a glutinous octave-unison of clarinet and bassoon.

Does this, in your opinion constitute the broadcasting of obscene material and should I communicate with Mrs Whitehouse?

Yours, etc.,
'Disgusted'.

Dear 'Disgusting of Manchester',
Such distressing cases are all too frequent. My own particular *betes noires* are the Mozart Requiem on clarinets instead of basset horns and the alto saxophone part of *Belshazzar's Feast* on the cor anglais. Indeed, I have it from the very lips of the man himself (Sir William Walton, I mean, not Belshazzar) that he really wanted the saxophone, and the cor anglais is only a makeshift alternative part for the most ill equipped amateur orchestra. The LSQ once appeared on a STV chat show with Mary Whitehouse, and she seemed most sympathetic to the cause of the saxophone, provided that the alto is played side saddle, not between the thighs.

Naturally, the root cause of all this is economic, one of the prime, ever-recurring instances being the orchestras who try to book one saxophonist to play both the soprano and tenor solos in Ravel's *Bolero*. Such unnatural practices should indeed be exposed; please continue to send in complaints to CASS. When we have accumulated enough evidence, a prosecution under the Trades Descriptions Act may be possible.

Uncle Paul

TRAINING THE LITTLE FINGERS FOR THEIR BIG JOB

Now that the Boehm system clarinet is used exclusively in nearly every country of the world, it is a continual source of amazement to me that so many student players do not make full use of the little finger keys.

Most of the pupils who come to me at Kneller Hall have been playing for as least two years, yet during their first lesson, when I assess how I can best help them, many perform prodigious feats of sliding and key-jumping when a simple L-R-L or R-L-R movement is all that is necessary. 'Try that arpeggio of G major using a right B', I say, and a trembling little finger waves uncertainly in the air, to come crashing down on right C sharp and wedge itself painfully under the E flat key.

To another new pupil, who has just rushed exuberantly up and down a chromatic scale with the usual fingering, I might say, 'Now play it again starting on right E'. Beads of perspiration stand out on his forehead as he goes cross-eyed looking down the instrument to clamp his right little finger on this gleaming, hardly ever touched key. Off we go: E, then a grace note to G as his left little finger makes a wild swipe at left F, and slips off that most elusive of keys: G sharp, mingling with a howl of pain as his right little finger's jab at F sharp impales the G sharp key under his finger nail. I can imagine him, after the lesson, sayng to his friends, 'My Professor is a sadistic fiend, who makes me play everything with the wrong fingerings. Everyone knows chromatic scales ALWAYS start with left E and that the fingering for B over the break is left little finger!'

Having revealed this deficiency in the pupil's technique, I tell him something of the history of the clarinet's development, while he massages his maltreated little fingers. I invariably finish by pointing out that the purpose of our benefactor, Klosé, in inventing the Boehm system was not to devise a means of torture for Kneller Hall pupils, but was actually to make certain passages EASIER to play! If this revelation is received with ill-concealed scepticism, I sometimes resort to sarcasm, such as: 'Perhaps you'd better trot along to the Instrument Stores and hand in you Boehm system. I'll give you a note to the curator of the Museum, and he'll pick out a nice simple system for you; better still, how about a snazzy six-key job in boxwood? They produce a lovely sweet tone if you can cut your reeds to the right shape, and once you get the cross-fingerings sorted out ... etc., etc.'

However, to come to the real point of this article. My remedy for all this is to teach the pupils three short passages known as 'HARVEY'S FINGER TWISTERS'. The fingerings are not, of course, the best to use if such passages occur in a piece, but are intended to train the little fingers to hit any required key instantly and accurately.

I have these three symphonies for rattling keys (idea for another article: *The Clarinet as a Percussion Instrument*) written out on a large sheet of cardboard and prominently displayed in my room. Then, for the rest of the course, whenever a pupil botches up a little finger key sequence, I merely give a resigned sigh and reach out for the Finger Twister Card.

My reward comes, after a year of laughing politely at such quips as, 'I think you've got a right hand B in your bonnet, Sir!' when I am passing the Pupils' dormitory block and an anonymous clarinet bell is poked through an upstairs window, intoning a fluent Finger Twister, rounded off with the first two notes of *Colonel Bogey*.

It's a difficult angle to see at, but I'm pretty certain the second note of the rebellious descending minor third was a RIGHT HAND E!

6 The Saxophone

TECHNICAL ARTICLES ON THE SAXOPHONE

This collection of articles emphasises the breadth of the subject. The bald title 'The Saxophone' suggests that we are dealing with a single instrument, but the reality is at least ten individual sets of problems; sopranino, alto, tenor, baritone, bass and the F/C family as well, not to mention the various different makes!

SOME THOUGHTS ON THE SAXOPHONE

Did you ever read Artie Shaw's autobiography, 'The Trouble With Cinderella'? Although my copy seems to have disappeared, I remember the subtitle was 'An Outline of Identity'. That is how I would like to start this piece, as I'm sometimes assailed by doubts as to whether I'm a clarinettist who also plays saxophone and composes, or a saxophonist who plays clarinet and composes, or a composer who plays clarinet and saxophone, or just an all round dilettante!

However, let me tell you how it all came about. Scene: The bandroom of the Empire Theatre, Sheffield. Date: 1949. (I remember the year because the show playing that week was called 'Naughty Nudes of 1949'). Fourteen-year-old Harvey is about to receive the first (and only) saxophone lesson of his life.

I'd been studying clarinet for two years with Billy Tomlinson, the clarinet and alto player at the Empire, who was a very fine clarinettist and teacher, but who had an awful mental block about the saxophone, although he'd played it twice nightly for twenty years or so. Unknown to him, I'd been hanging around the local music store every Saturday morning since I was eleven, tearing up and down all the woodwind instruments, including saxophone, until being forcibly ejected, dusty but happy, at closing time. He'd decided I was now proficient enough on clarinet to dep (sub) for him at the Empire, so he'd signed me up in the Musicians' Union and it only remained for me to gain the minimum acquaintance with that necessary evil, the saxophone.

There it crouched, in the darkest corner of the bandroom, its ancient case blackened and charred from the explosion of an incendiary bomb which had dropped into the bowels of the theatre during the blitz eight years previously. 'There's t'sax, lad,' said Billy, "ere's a fingerin' chart and t'parts for t'show. Tha's on at 7.30. I'll be in t'pub if tha wants me.' His pedagogical duties thus discharged, Billy beat a hasty retreat to the stage door pub, before he had to hear his pet clarinet pupil prostituting himself on the devil's instrument!

I never dared admit to Billy that I LIKED playing the saxophone, as he would either have burst into tears or assaulted me physically!

A few months later I did an audition on clarinet for the National Youth Orchestra of Great Britain, and was accepted. One of the concerts included Bizet's *L'Arlésienne*, and with my Professional experience on the saxophone, it naturally fell to my lot to play the well-known solo, though how 'Naughty Nudes of 1949' qualified me for this, I never fathomed! Armed with an elderly alto borrowed from the friendly neighbourhood music store, I commenced my career as an orchestral saxophonist, doughnut firmly into the bell for the bottom C, using the vibrato I'd developed for my clandestine activities as a jazz clarinettist. (Billy didn't like jazz either, and he equated vibrato on the clarinet with smallpox or the Black Death!)

Then came quite a long gap in my relationship with the saxophone, as I won a Scholarship to the Royal College of Music (on clarinet, of course) did my National Service with the Band of the Irish Guards (on clarinet) and then got my first proper job in the Scottish National Orchestra (on bass clarinet). It was only when I returned to London to freelance in 1960 that I bought an alto and started to do orchestral saxophone work again. I assiduously practised *L'Arlésienne, Harry Janos, Pictures from an Exhibition, 'Job'*, etc. Then I bought a tenor and practised *Romeo and Juliet, Bolero* and Vaughan Williams' Sixth. By the mid 60s I was playing these and other such parts with most of the London Orchestras and had a pretty fair monopoly of all the BBC Symphony saxophone work.

I even got to play the alto solo in Britten's *Our Hunting Fathers* in (wait for it) yes, CARNEGIE HALL. (That place on W. 56th St and 7th Ave, you know). Then, in 1969, I met Christopher Gradwell in a clarinet group, and he asked me to play soprano in a saxophone quartet he was forming. 'Well,' I thought, 'it won't last long, but it'll be useful practice on the soprano.' I had a soprano under the bed, on which I'd played a few Boleros and the odd show. So I went along to Christopher's quartet, and practically overnight, I found myself Leader of the London Saxophone Quartet, leaping on and off aeroplanes, eyes bulging, beads of perspiration on my forehead as I struggled through soprano parts written for Marcel Mule, announcing programmes in French and Spanish, and trying to learn to play the soprano properly at the same time! What a traumatic experience for an unoffending clarinettist!

So what is my present position? Although anyone reading this article will presumably equate me with the LSQ, my basic bread and butter job is teaching clarinet at Kneller Hall, for which I am much more qualified than teaching saxophone. However, my composition and arranging activities have become more biased towards the saxophone, probably because I feel the clarinet has plenty of composers writing for it, while my efforts are of more use to the saxophone.

Well, this article is not intended to be my autobiography, but I wanted to sketch in my background to show that I approach the saxophone with no preconceived ideas from any teacher, never having had one! I had a very good training on the clarinet, but this does not necessarily mean that I play saxophone with the strangled sound of the straight clarinettist trying to blow it for the first time. Marcel Mule once said to me, 'You 'ave a very fine Quatuor, M'sieu 'Arvey, which amazes me, because not only are you all clarinettists, but you are also ENGLEESH!' As I explained to le maitre at the time, I play clarinet with an ideal doubler's embouchure; that is, with the bottom lip turned out, and not much over the bottom teeth. All the tension is in my top lip and cheeks, supported by lots of diaphragm pressure. This embouchure transfers successfully to the saxophone, with some modification of the mouth and throat cavity. I've read everything I could find about the saxophone and experimented a great deal, especially with the soprano. Over recent years I've come to some conclusions about the instrument, which I've decided to commit to paper for the first time in this article. They may not be original; I just don't know, though I have never read anything about this myself. They may not be of any practical value, but I've become quite obsessed about it lately, and they may provide food for thought in some areas where it might be possible to follow them up. So here we go.

Over recent years I've become more and more convinced that we're all ('classical' saxophonists, that is) playing on the wrong family of saxophones. Every book or biographical note on Adolphe Sax always states that he invented TWO families of saxophones: the B flat/E flat group for military band use, and the C/F group for orchestral use. Why, then, are we struggling to play concerti, orchestral solos and chamber music on instruments designed for robust outdoor use in military bands? I know that many of the finest saxophonists can play very softly at the bottom of the instrument, but how many years of practice has it taken them to achieve this? Nobody can tell me they find it easy, even now, though it may sound easy. The worst clarinettist will always be able to play low notes softer than the best saxophonist; I know its the cylindrical v. conical bore, but should the difference be as great?

The answer, as always, must lie in economics. The vast majority of saxophone purchasers want them for jazz playing, so naturally the manufacturers concentrate all their efforts into the B flat/E flat family, which are obviously the best for producing a jazz sound. But why should this totally exclude the C/F family, with its more refined and centred sound?

Consider the case of the trumpet; every orchestral trumpet player I work with nowadays carries an enormous case containing B flat, C, D, piccolo E flat and F trumpets. I questioned one about this recently, and he said they use whichever size suits the type of music to be played. Most orchestral first trumpets use the C instrument most of the time to play parts written for B flat, because of its smaller but more concentrated sound. I understand horn and tuba players are up to similar tricks. The manufacturers don't say 'Jazz trumpeters only use the B flat trumpet, so that's the only one we'll make.'

So why don't saxophonists start agitating to have the C/F family manufactured once again? The so called 'C melody' or C tenor was, of course, popular in the 1920s, but for the wrong reason; merely for the convenience of playing off concert pitch song copies. But there are still a few about, and Chris Gradwell bought one recently. I was immediately struck by its mellow sound and ease of production compared with the B flat tenor.

C sopranos have also been made; possibly to play oboe parts in military bands. I bought one recently; a dirty, silver plated, geriatric looking thing; keys only to top E flat, no button or long B flat, no articulated G sharp or left little finger keys linkage and no chromatic F sharp key. How basic can you get? No maker was willing to admit to its manufacture on its un-numbered, unornamented bell. I threw away a revolting mouthpiece which clung tenaciously to its stubby little neck, and managed to fit my own on with the help of lots of paper padding. Then I blew it . . . at last . . . the sound . . . what a soprano saxophone was meant to sound like . . . a sound I've carried in my head these last ten years, without ever being able to reproduce it on any B flat soprano. But it was very flat; my Selmer mouthpiece had much too long a shank. Never mind . . . where's the hacksaw? The blade's rusty, but who cares? Gibbering with insane excitement I attack my mouthpiece shank with a rusty hacksaw until its short enough. I strapped my wife to the piano stool and got out the pile of baroque oboe music which I have always planned to use for a great world-shaking soprano recital, but never thought the sound was right before. Now I played through the lot, having to concentrate to use only side key B flat and all the other basic fingerings, and I've never enjoyed playing any saxophone more! My four modern, expensive B flat sopranos lay unwanted, gleaming with gold laquer, gnashing their complicated modern mechanism with jealousy.

Next morning I looked at my C soprano in the cold light of day. It's really pretty basic, but I could have the mechanism modernised. But no . . . further experimenting brought another revelation. The modern saxophone has too many mechanical refinements, especially the articulated G sharp. Why has the full Boehm clarinet never really caught on? One reason is because you lose the long top F and F sharp fingerings, not being able to open the G sharp key when your right hand's down. But its possible to get round this on the clarinet by half holing with the 3rd finger left hand; impossible on the saxophone, of course. Let's see what happens on this unarticulated G sharp saxophone . . . good heavens . . . a lovely clear harmonic top F . . . and here's an E. No need to have any more horrid little holes made in the neck; I hate them; nasty thin, unstable, wheezy notes. I had a soprano with keys up to top G once; never used them and got rid of it as soon as possible. Harmonics are always better. I'm sure all that drilling of a soprano's thin, delicate little neck can do the tone of the rest of the instrument no good. So we've disposed of articulated G sharps and holes for top notes . . . what's next?

Dash down to Buffet's for John Coppen to drill a bleed hole in the left hand 1st finger plate. This is something he thought of to improve middle D on my B flat soprano; a sort of third octave hole, like the oboe has. It works very well, and you can play all the notes down to B flat in the upper register, giving a useful alternative timbre to the usual lower register fingerings. Now, on the bass clarinet, the bleed hole is used to facilitate harmonics. Maybe it will have the same effect on the C soprano... yes, it does; with the combination of bleed hole and unarticulated G sharp, I'm finding some unheard of harmonic fingerings! I keep looking at my gleaming B flat sopranos, and fingering my rusty hacksaw thoughtfully...

No, never mind them; the priority now is to get a C/F quartet going. I've got a C soprano and Chris has a C tenor. I once blew an F alto, and again thought what a lovely sound it was, but, like a fool, I didn't buy it. However, one will be found somewhere. The big problem is the F baritone. I don't know anyone who's ever seen one. I know Schoenberg wrote for bass saxophone in C in *Von Heute Auf Morgen* as I've played the part on baritone, but that was obviously because he couldn't be bothered to transpose the part.

No, the F baritone is the stumbling block. This is where I must leave you, with wild plans fermenting in my brain to procure a baritone body and a set of keys from Buffets and get Ted Planas to shrink the body and cut down the keys. Or perhaps my mother could knit one if I buy her enough wool! Maybe I should stick to the clarinet, or take up pig farming before it all gets too much for me! I'll let you know how I get on, anyway.

WRITING FOR THE SAXOPHONE

Adolphe Sax, the inventor of the saxophone, would heartily agree with my first point, which is to exhort composers to think not only of that prima donna, the alto, but to consider the saxophones as a family, a true consort of instruments. The saxophone quartet (soprano, alto, tenor, baritone) has enjoyed such a remarkable upsurge of popularity over the last ten years, and in particular since the World Saxophone Congress was held at the Royal College of Music in 1976, that it can safely be assumed that all four instruments are now readily available for orchestral use, as well as in regular quartets. The two extremities, the E flat Sopranino and B flat bass are still rather rare, but can often be produced if you know which player you are writing for.

As to writing for the instrument, one great truth holds good for all sizes; when the part is transposed to saxophone pitch it should look like a good *oboe* part. One would not be widely admired by the oboe fraternity if one wrote a passage commencing on a pianissimo bottom B or B flat. This is because the oboe is a conical bore woodwind instrument, unlike the cylindrical clarinet, on which nothing is easier than to commence on soft bottom notes. Now the saxophone is the most conical of all woodwind instruments, so this problem is even more evident in the case of the alto and tenor especially. The soprano is not quite so bad, owing to its smaller bore, and the baritone is designed in such a way as to favour the bottom notes at the expense of the top, as that is the part of its range composers will obviously wish to utilise the most. But even so, you must bear in mind the large volume of breath required to sustain low baritone notes, and not hold them on too long. The bottom four notes on alto and tenor (C sharp, C, B and B flat) can of course be used, providing you realise that they will be big, loud sounds. Run down to them, do not jump down to them, and, above all, do not start passages on them, especially softly. It may seem to you that I am obsessed with these four notes, but I assure you that sensible use of them is what makes the difference between a good and a bad saxophone part. Any professional saxophonist will happily do his best to play up to an octave above the conventional range on harmonics; he may not always make it, but he will have a go. But ask him to play a pianissimo bottom B flat and you have made an enemy for life! The most quoted alto saxophone solo, Bizet's *L'Arlesienne,* is a nightmare to play properly, because it slurs down to two bottom C's at the end. Anyone can honk these notes out loudly in the privacy of their own boudoir, but to play them softly with the red light on, or in a concert hall is what sorts out the men from the boys. To this end one sometimes resorts to the use of a 'Doughnut', a sort of cloth mute. Composers are sometimes misled by this, however, equating it with a brass mute, which changes the tone quality of the whole instrument, since on brass instruments, all notes sound through the bell, thus passing through the mute. A saxophone mute only affects notes on the bottom half of the tube (about G-C) and the bottom B and B flat cannot be produced with it in, as they have to sound through the bell. So there is no point in specifically writing for a mute; it is only a player's device to produce softer bottom C sharps and C's.

The main range of the instrument, from bottom D to top F, has no particular problems, apart from intonation characteristics on certain notes, which are up to the player to sort out. Complete chromatic facility is available throughout this range. We then enter the *altissimo* register, and at least another octave is obtainable on harmonics. Most modern saxohpones have a key for top F sharp, so that is quite an easy note; then there are two rather unpredictable notes, G and G sharp, and from A upwards another sixth or so is possible, but easier in jumps rather than runs. But it must be borne in mind that this is the realm of the specialist saxophonist. If you are writing an orchestral part with no particular player in mind, it is very likely that the part will be played by a clarinettist, who has not had the time to explore these harmonics, in the way that specialist saxophonists in France and America do. Fingering charts exist for these notes, but these are not enough; the range has to be built up by harmonic exercises on the fundamentals of the closed tube; the upper partials of the saxophone are much harder to control than those of the clarinet. So, when venturing to write above the conventional range, it is essential to consult the player one has in mind.

The most rewarding field for a composer to explore is undoubtedly the saxophone quartet. The most essential advice here is to warn against using string quartet textures. Always bear in mind that the sonority of a saxophone quartet is very much richer than strings, and overwriting is a constant danger. A good example is the Glazounov *Quartet;* a delightful work musically, but obviously conceived as if written for string quartet, and consequently most wearing to the ear if it is performed in its entirety. There is no shortage of original repertoire of the most demanding technical standard, but this country now abounds with amateur and student quartets who urgently need material of a more approachable nature. This is the market which I would advise composers to consider, as music of this sort is more likely to find a publisher and be more widely performed.

Ranges and transpositions of the Saxophone Quartet

The same advice applies to multiphonics, and other contemporary effects. Many of these are possible on the saxophone, but there is no standard practice as yet. They vary considerably between different instruments and different players. If you examine the contemporary solo literature for saxophone, you will see most multiphonics notated as to fingering, and these will be the fingerings which work on the saxophone of the dedicatee, perhaps Jean-Marie Londeix of Bordeaux, or Daniel Deffayet of Paris, or one of the American University saxophonists. So again, it is essential to consult a player who is making a specialized study of these techniques.

THE WAGNERIAN SAXOPHONE

In the third act of Wagner's *Tristan and Isolde*, Tristan lies wounded in his castle in Brittany. His faithful servant, Kurvenal, has sent a ship to bring Isolde from Cornwall, and throughout the first part of the act the two men await the coming of the ship. The only other character to appear in this scene is a shepherd, whose 'ancient and mournful piping' first wakes Tristan from his feverish slumber. Kurvenal instructs the shepherd to keep watch for Isolde's ship, and to 'pipe lustily and merrily' when the ship comes in sight.

This the shepherd agrees to do, returning to his vantage point on the cliffs, from whence his mournful tune is heard intermittently, signifying that the ship is not yet to be seen. This section is played by an offstage cor anglais, which instrument ideally suits the character of the shepherd's first tune.

Eventually the shepherd sights the ship on the horizon, and the character of his piping changes completely. First a fanfare-like figure to catch the attention of Tristan and Kurvenal:
(Concert Pitch)

Then the merry tune which the shepherd had promised:

Kurvenal runs to the watch tower to follow the shoreward progress of the ship through dangerous reefs, his anxiety reflected by the shepherd's staccato variation on his tune:

4 Times

When both see the ship safe in the harbour, the shepherd pipes his merry tune for the last time. This whole section from the shepherd's first sighting of the ship gave Wagner much doubt as to what instrument to employ in the wings. In the full score he continues the part in cor anglais pitch, but says in a footnote that the cor anglais will be neither loud enough nor jolly enough. He suggests a 'powerful, even rough, folk instrument, of a natural naivete'.

His further suggestion, to try a homemade wooden instrument of the Alphorn variety has rarely been adopted, probably because the speed of the variation figure really requires a woodwind instrument. The choice of many Opera Houses has often been the Tarogato; a Hungarian folk instrument which may be described either as a conical bored clarinet, or a wooden soprano saxophone.

However, the Vienna Opera first hit on the idea of using a soprano saxophone, and this season the English National Opera have decided to follow suit and engaged me as the offstage shepherd for their new production of *Tristan and Isolde*, which I am still playing a couple of times each week. Although the Musical Director made the decision to use a soprano saxophone, that has still left me with scope for experimentation. I have to bear in mind that I am not supposed to be the leader of the London Saxophone Quartet, striving to produce a cultivated sound, in tune, with delicate articulation. I am a Breton shepherd, who has never seen a note of written music in his life, has never attended a saxophone clinic, and has probably never even heard of Marcel Mule (well, it IS supposed to be in the twelfth century!) I am overjoyed at having sighted the ship bearing my master's beloved, and want to convey the glad tidings to the two gents up at the castle.

At first I played for safety, using my normal B flat soprano which I use in the quartet. This brings the passage into D major, which lies well for saxophone fingering, the variation coming out thus:

4 Times

However, after the first dress rehearsal, the conductor said I was beginning to make it sound too easy: it would be better if every note seemed a struggle! I contemplated using a harder reed, but decided instead to switch to C soprano. I rewrote the part down a tone, and in the concert pitch key (see first three examples) it is technically more of a struggle to keep the speed up. Also the C soprano has a wilder, more trumpet-like sound, possibly closer to the Breton shepherd idea.

Now this kind of experimentation gets a grip on you, and at the last performance I passed some of my waiting time in the band room writing out the part down another minor third, with a view to enlivening the last couple of performances by playing it on . . . yes, you guessed it . . . the ultimate deterrent . . . the dreaded E flat sopranino saxophone! On this instrument the part lies nearly all in the bottom register, so it has a more nasal quality:

4 Times

It may be that the sopranino is nearest to Wagner's intention, as all the notes in this passage are fundamentals, and would the shepherd's pipe have overblown octaves?

So there I sit in the wings at every performance, with three instruments and three parts in different keys, agonizing over which one to play. I feel quite close to Wagner; just the assistant conductor and me in the wings, Tristan and Kurvenal on the stage; I am waiting for some sign from the Master as to which instrument he prefers. Who knows, perhaps at the final performance a spotlight will fall on my head!

7 Reviews

My purpose in writing reviews has always been to disseminate information, not to criticize. So many young players (and some older ones, for that matter) seem to be incredibly ignorant of what is going on anywhere but in their own particular little sphere. Who is composing for their instrument; who is giving recitals; who is lecturing, teaching and writing about it.

I include the appreciation and obituary of Gordon Jacob, as although they are not reviews, they provide vital information for any wind player.

My review of Colin Bradbury's Victorian album, purporting to have been written by Henry Lazarus, is a particular favourite of mine. I once met a very old flute player who had been a pupil at Kneller Hall when Lazarus was still teaching there, and he told me that the great man really was a bit on the egotistical side, as I have portrayed him. Unfortunately, I never wrote any more of the promised articles by great wind players of the past. I remember I planned one by Anton Stadler, about his composer friend, Wolfgang Wotsisname.

One day, perhaps!

THE WOODWIND MUSIC OF GORDON JACOB

Gordon Percival Septimus Jacob, CBE, musD, FRCM, Hon, RAM., b: London, 1895. Professor of Composition and Orchestration, Royal College of Music, 1924–1967.

Whenever I am in the throes of orchestrating a work, I like to have everything on my desk in its appointed place; paper, ruler, pens, pencils, ashtray, cup of tea, etc. . . . and, readily available on my left, a certain slim, green book. Very faded and dog-eared now, bearing the ringed pattern of twenty years' tea cups. Its title . . . *Orchestral Technique* by Gordon Jacob. A masterpiece of concise and practical information, to which I constantly refer.

Dr Gordon Jacob, CBE, the famous British composer, conducting Redbridge Symphony Orchestra at Ilford Town Hall.

I remember, in my long departed youth, passing the audition for the National Youth Orchestra with the Tartini-Jacob Concertino, and was recently delighted to learn that there is now an arrangement by Dr Jacob for clarinet choir.

Last year, June Emerson sent me a copy of the Dorian Variations for alto saxophone, which I reviewed adding my usual paragraph about writing a saxophone quartet, which is now a reflex action when reviewing new music . . . ie, 'Mr Beethoven's 9th Symphony is an impressive piece of work; however, now he's got it off his chest, let's hope he will get down to his long-awaited saxophone quartet!' Imagine my delight when this actually worked. (With Jacob, I mean, not Beethoven, though I'm working on that). Yes, the London Saxophone Quartet is now preparing for the first performance of Gordon Jacob's new four movement work, which is to be published by June Emerson.

About the same time I started to rehearse the Kneller Hall

Clarinet Choir in his Introduction and Rondo, which will be the main work in our next concert.

What should arrive one morning but his Five Pieces for unaccompanied clarinet, just published by Oxford University Press.

Then, just before Christmas, my overworked postman delivered a set of Paul Brodie's brilliant new *Music Minus One* albums for alto saxophone. One of the items was by . . . yes, you guessed . . . his *Rhapsody*, originally for cor anglais and strings.

I began to feel that tingling in my two typing fingers which means a story coming on.

So I wrote to Dr Jacob at Saffron Walden, Essex, where he lives in tranquil 'retirement' (I MUST be joking!) and asked for a complete list of his woodwind music and any reminiscences of great woodwind players he has known. The full list of works would fill this issue and half the next, so I'll content myself with quoting the most interesting recollections of players, using Dr Jacob's own words:

'Frederick 'Jack' Thurston (clarinet)

He was a fellow student of mine at the Royal College of Music in the years following World War 1. I remember timing how long he could play without taking a breath. He walked about the room improvising for a minute and a quarter, with a steady crescendo through the last 30 seconds or so. I wrote my Clarinet Quintet for him and the Griller Quartet.

Leon Goossens (oboe)

Premiered my 1st. Oboe Concerto with the Halle Orchestra under Beecham n 1935. Asked me to write an oboe quartet which he played at the Wigmore Hall with the Philharmonic Trio in 1938 and 39. He told me not to worry about whether passages were playable. If a composer wrote anything within the instrument's compass the player's job was to play it (I'm happy to report that Dr Jacob is the last composer in the world to follow this rash advice! — P.H.) I also wrote my 2nd Oboe Concerto for him which he first played in Russia. I remember an embarrassing occasion when he and I were appearing at the same concert, but were not required to be on the platform at the same time. I had forgotten to bring the detachable buttons of my white waistcoat, so I borrowed his for my conducting turn, hastily returning them for his appearance. On another occasion he was playing Concerto No 1 and I was conducting on a rostrum which produced agonised squeaks at my slightest movement. (Good thing it wasn't a clarinet concerto — P.H.)

Archie Camden (bassoon)
I was having a wash in the Gent's at the RCM when AC came in and said, 'I wish you'd write a Concerto for me.' I naturally jumped at this suggestion, and in 1947 he played my bassoon concerto at a Prom. When I was staying at his house one day he suddenly turned on the radio. The Finale of Beethoven 4 was going on, and immediately after the very fast bassoon solo he snapped it off, saying, 'I only wanted to hear how that bit came off.'

Terence McDonagh (oboe)
I wrote my Cor Anglais Rhapsody for him, also the Divertimento for Wind Octet at his request. I examined Wind Instruments for ARCM at one time, and I remember sight-reading tests as administered by Terry. 'One, two, three . . . off you go!' No time for looking at it beforehand; absolutely the right attitude for future orchestral players. I also remember his father, who played oboe in Henry Wood's orchestra at Queen's Hall many years ago.

Gareth Morris (flute)
My flute concerto was written for him and first played at a Prom in 1952. I remember him showing me a flute tutor not very efficiently translated from the original German. It had some very comic things in it, e.g. 'Exercises in chromatic quarts'.

John Francis (flute)
Some of my chamber works were written for him and his daughter Sarah, a fine oboist. A curious family ensemble, consisting of flute, oboe, harp and harpsichord existed at one time, and I was asked to write for this. It was a real challenge, and yielded some interesting effects in performance.

Evelyn Rothwell (Lady Barbirolli) (oboe)
My sonata and sonatina for oboe were written for her to play with Valda Aveling, hence my use of harpsichord in these works.

William Waterhouse (bassoon)
My smaller bassoon pieces were written for him. He demonstrated on the bassoon how to breathe in while playing, which seems to flout the second law of thermodynamics or something, but can be done.

I once, when a student, wrote a piece for flute, trumpet, side drum and piano, which caused my Composition Professor, Sir Charles Villiers Stanford, to growl something about 'impossible combinations'. Recently I wrote a Suite for the Kent Wind Society which has 50 flutes, 20 oboes, 40 clarinets, a forest of bassoons and brass to match (only 1 or 2 bass clarinets, though!) It sounded well in the Chapter House at Canterbury when it was packed with audience. One reason for having audiences at concerts is to provide about six square feet of sound-absorbing material per person.'

Well, what can I say to sum up all that? Isn't it nice to know that not all composers die in misery at the age of thirty five?

Isn't is nice for us woodwind nuts to know that somebody, somewhere, loves us?

Isn't is nice to know that Gordon Jacob, b: London, 1895, is still writing delightful music for us in Saffron Walden?

GORDON PERCIVAL SEPTIMUS JACOB, CBE, DMus, FRCM, Hon.RAM (1895-1984)

The recent death of Gordon Jacob at 88 years severs one of our last links with the dignified age of Elgar and of Sir Charles Villiers Stanford, who was Dr Jacob's principal teacher at the Royal College of Music. But he was by no means a composer who lived on past achievements, being prolific to the end; our youngest clarinet pupils are even now being introduced to his music in the shape of the new Associated Board exam pieces which were among his last commissions. My own first recollection of listening to music with any degree of attention and interest is as a small boy in the early 1940s. At that time, during the darker days of the Second World War, one of the greatest morale boosters was a zany radio show called *ITMA* (these initials actually stood for 'It's That Man Again', referring to Tommy Handley, a very popular comedian). Each show featured a musical interlude played by the BBC Variety Orchestra, most of which were brilliant arrangements of folk tunes by Gordon Jacob, which became popular in their own right, apart from the show. So I counted myself very privileged when I got to know Dr Jacob in later life, and gave the first performances of four of his saxophone works.

In 1973 I was helping to plan the London Saxophone Quartet's repertoire for the following year's World Saxophone Congress in Bordeaux, and approached Dr Jacob with a commission for a quartet. He was delighted with the idea, and produced the work, which is now well-known to saxophone quartets all over the world, in record time. It has four movements: *Allegro moderato; Scherzo and Trio alla musette; Adagio molto* and *Alla marcia, con spirito.*

After the Congress the LSQ recorded the Jacob quartet for Transatlantic Records, which has since gone out of business, but I am delighted to be able to report that the original recording is once more available, on cassette, from RONCORP Inc., P.O. Box 724, Cherry Hill, New Jersey, USA, 08003.

The next World Saxophone Congress was to be held in London, hosted by the London Saxophone Quartet; this came about in 1976 at the Royal College of Music, and as the accompanying group at the opening concert was to be the Band of the Irish Guards (which happened to be the Band in which I did my own military service back in the 1950s) I again approached Dr Jacob. He came up with *Miscellanies* for alto saxophone and wind orchestra: a delightful suite of seven pieces: *Scalic Prelude, Folk Song, Moto Perpetuo, Interlude, Gavotte, Dirge* and *March.* The saxophone part lies within the conventional range, and is an ideal solo work for a promising young saxophonist (or, indeed, for a middle-aged quartet soprano player who doesn't have much time to practise the alto!) The band voicing has the distinctive Jacob master touch, but I have since performed the work several times with the composer's own piano reduction, which is equally effective.

In 1979 the tenth anniversary of the London Saxophone Quartet was upon us, and we planned a commemorative concert at St John's, Smith Square. Of all the new works which had been written for us over the ten years, the Jacob quartet stood out as the most successful, so I diffidently suggested a second quartet. Again four masterly movements arrived: *Moderato, poco pomposo-Allegro; Adagio, Allegro moderato;* and *Larghetto-Allegro.* We gave the first performance at St John's, and subsequently recorded it for the BBC. Unfortunately this is the only Jacob saxophone work not yet published.

Dr Jacob wrote his last saxophone work in 1981; I was due to give a concert with Catherine Shrubshall, one of my most promising students at the time, although I had written some duets for alto and tenor for her myself, I asked Dr Jacob for something for soprano and alto, as these were the instruments which we played the best.

The resulting *Duo* for soprano and alto saxophone is a gem among woodwind duet literature: an *Allegro* which is a model of two-part counterpoint; an expressive *Adagio;* and, finally, a set of

Variations on an old five-finger exercise from Smallwood's Pianoforte Tutor, which Dr Jacob told me was the first thing he ever played, back in about 1902! We gave the first performance of the *Duo* at Kensington Institute, with further performances at Theobald's College and the Middlesex Polytechnic.

What is not widely known is that Dr Jacob had lost the sight of one eye some years ago, so wrote out the scores of all these (and many other) works with the use of only one eye. I copied the parts of both quartets and the duo from his original score, and was often aware of the difficulty he experienced in writing the noteheads accurately on the lines or spaces, so that much checking between us was necessary of the notes he intended.

All wind players have much to thank Gordon Jacob for his other works for solo wind instruments, chamber groups and wind band are far too numerous to list here, but they are, without exception, beautifully written and a joy to play and listen to. Yet it is not only for his own compositions that we have cause to be grateful, but for his contribution to the development of the work of innumerable younger English composers who studied with him during almost half a century as a professor at the Royal College of Music. Although I was not fortunate enough to have been his student myself, his definitive book on orchestration, *Orchestral Technique*, is invariably at my elbow whenever I set pen to manuscript paper.

I am sure that the long life and prolific works of Gordon Jacob will be remembered and appreciated for as long as the playing of musical instruments flourishes around the world.

JOHN DENMAN: Clarinettist
and a Great Musical Score

Last year Mr Denman made a remarkable discovery in a private London music collection; a score of Louis Spohr's rarely performed Second Clarinet Concerto in E flat, Opus 57. This was in the handwriting of Henry Lazarus, signed by him and dated 1833; twenty-three years after the work's composition and first performance in Frankenhausen, at which the composer conducted, and the soloist was the legendary Johann Hermstedt, of Sonderhausen, for whom Spohr wrote all his clarinet works.

This Concerto had never been recorded, due to the disappearance of the authentic orchestral material. Mr Denman has now rectified this by recording it with the Sadlers Wells Orchestra, conducted by Hazel Vivienne, on Unicorn Records. It is coupled with an earlier rarity; Concerto Number 3 in E flat by Karl Stamitz, composer for Josef Beer (1744–1811).

Dr Stephen K. Johnston,
Shenandoah College and Conservatory of Music, Winchester, Virginia

In Paul Harvey's article in the September 1973 issue, 'John Denman: Clarinettist and a Great Musical Score', it was reported that Sophr wrote all of his clarinet works for J. S. Hermstedt. This information is incorrect inasmuch as Spohr composed in 1804 or 1805 a concert-piece consisting of a recitative, an adagio, and a rondo for a clarinettist named Tretbach, a friend in the Brunswick orchestra; the first two movements were utilized later in the Violin Concerto, Opus 28. A review of a concert in the *Allgemeine musikalische Zeitung* notes that the work was performed in Hildburghausen in 1821.

Mr Harvey also stated that Spohr's Second Clarinet Concerto had not been recorded previously because of '... the disappearance of the authentic orchestral material'. It should be noted that I am in possession of a microfilm of a holograph of the score. The neat manuscript is in the holdings of the Gesellschaft der Musikfreunde in Vienna (VII 5207), and was utilized in a dissertation on the clarinet concertos of Spohr.

TRAGIC RESULT OF THE GREAT
SPOHR CONTROVERSY
W.W. EUROPED COMMITS RITUAL SUICIDE
ON STEPS OF SPOHR SOCIETY BUILDING

Women and children ran screaming from the forecourt of the British Spohr Society today, as Paul Harvey, W.W.'s discredited European Editor, disembowelled himself with a contrabass clarinet spike on the historic marble steps.
LAST WORDS
His last words, agonisingly hissed through a blood-spattered embouchure, were: 'I did not check my facts!' This is believed to refer to certain statements he made in the September issue of W.W. concerning Spohr's second Clarinet Concerto; later proved to be erroneous by a correspondent in the December issue.
FEELS RESPONSIBLE
John Denman, believed by his many disciples to be a reincarnation of Johan Hermstedt, choked back a sob as he told reporters at 'Sonderhausen' his South-London home: 'I somehow

feel responsible for this tragedy. I gave Paul the facts over the telephone, and was eating a toffee at the time.'

GREATEST WORK

Harvey, portly 38-year-old Yorkshireman, leaves a widow, one daughter, eight clarinets and five saxophones. At the funeral, in the Kneller Hall Chapel, John Denman and Fred Tretbach will perform selections from *Graded Study-Duets for two clarinets*, considered by connoisseurs to be Harvey's greatest work.

RECORD REVIEW
'Clarinet Carnival' — Mark Walton

Chalumeau Records, 9 Upland Road, London SE22 EBY001

I think a new era of unashamed virtuosity may soon be upon us. I do hope so; when I was a student this sort of thing was frowned upon. One of my composition professors at the Royal College of Music once wrote on my report: 'If he could stop writing display pieces for the clarinet he might be quite a good composer!' But I never saw any reason to stop, which is probably why I've been passed over again in the Birthday Honours list.

Many clarinettists have been saying recently. 'If only the clarinet had a Jim Galway to capture the public's interest!' John Denman started a trend that way, but has been seduced by the Academic Arcadia of Arizona. I think Mark Walton could be our Jim Galway; he only needs to get his keys gold plated and work a bit harder on his New Zealand accent. 'Good on yer, cobbers. Did I ever tell yez how I got started in a didgeridoo band in the slums of Christchurch? Here's a fantastically difficult set of variations on Maori Melodies, written by my chief arranger, Paul Harvey. He'll be selling copies at the door after the concert.'

Yes, what the lad needs is a good manager; I think I'll draw up an exclusive contract right away; I always fancied the Svengali bit; it's easier than having to play yourself! Anyway, all clarinettists should buy the record; its a great incentive to practise!

A RECITAL AND
NEW MUSIC REVIEW

Hard by the ancient Tower of London, the Parish Church of St Olave is the venue for a number of interesting lunch hour recitals, a striking feature of which is the provision of a modest but wholesome lunch for only fifty pence. (This has to be the best value in London!) It was a new experience for me to sit in a well-worn pew of this beautiful old church, consuming curried spaghetti, cheese on toast, ginger cake and coffee. I was just wondering whether I could afford a second helping when the performers entered. Lunch hour concerts here have to be exactly timed so that the audience can return to their offices at two o'clock, so I had to forsake my gastronomic musings and concentrate on the music.

Stephen Pierce, who is Professor of Clarinet at the London College of Music, gave an immediate impression of a fine clear sound and a confident, even technique in the *Four Characteristic Pieces* of William Hurlstone. There was also evidence of a very well-rehearsed partnership with pianist William Blezard, especially in such flexible passages as the rubato sections of the *Intermezzo*. William Blezard then played two sharply contrasted piano solos, the quiet contemplative Debussy *Clair de Lune* bursting into the pianistic, ebullient Dohnanyi *Rhapsody*.

Stephen Pierce returned with his bass clarinet to give the first complete performance of William Blezard's Concertino, commissioned by Stephen Pierce for bass clarinet and strings. The composer played his own piano reduction on this occasion. This exciting new work was brilliantly played. Stephen Pierce's bass clarinet playing was extremely impressive, displaying a rich full sound in the low register, confident control and intonation of the altissimo and unusually clean articulation.

It struck me immediately that this Concertino is the only original work for bass clarinet that would have been suitable for this type of audience which consisted mainly of music-loving office workers. All the other works for bass clarinet which I have heard were written for Spaarny or Horak and were, without exception, written in a contemporary language incomprehensible to this type of audience. William Blezard's work, on the other hand, maintains interest throughout and passes through a wide gamut of moods while utilizing the full four-octave range very effectively. The composition is finely crafted by an experienced professional composer and is nicely balanced in form. The immediate audience appeal which the work evokes, however, must be attributed to its many attractive themes and developments.

The Blezard Concertino is in three movements and should really be classed as a concerto. The composer told me that he called it a concertino because of its light style. Personally, I think this reasoning points to a sad case of a composer being brainwashed by such epithets as 'conservative' and 'light' when actually his music is of much greater practical use to the performer and gives audiences more pleasure than much music which is considered 'serious' and 'worthwhile'. I would love to hear this work with strings and consider it to be just the kind of work which should be played by clarinettists to represent contemporary British composition.

The recital ended with Billy Amstell's *Stick O'Liquorice* for clarinet and piano. After not having heard this 1940s novelty piece for some twenty-five years, I had played it at several recitals last year. Lately it seems to have become 'the trend', however, as I have since heard it finishing some three other recitals! I think some publisher should think of republishing this piece because the audiences' reactions to it are always sensational. If it becomes even trendier and becomes 'everybody's encore piece, I can see two schools of thought arising as to an appropriate tempo for the music. Personally, I feel is should be a moderately paced, swingy little tune, not a top-speed Olympic record *Dizzy Fingers* type of tune.

The Pierce-Blezard speed of *Liquroice* certainly had a spectacular effect on one member of the audience who leaped out of his pew exclaiming 'Blimey, mate, I never thought I'd hear anything like that in church!' (or words to the effect) and proceeded to jump up and down in the aisle (Perhaps this reaction was actually the after effects of a surfeit of curried spaghetti). It occurred to me that, in times gone by, Messrs. Pierce and Blezard might well have been frogmarched away to the nearby Tower to be thrown into a deep, dark dungeon for causing people to enjoy themselves in church!

HARVEY RAISES LAZARUS!

Here is the first of a new series of exclusive articles by, and interviews with,great wind players of the past. This quite incredible presentaion is made possible by the teaming of reed instrumentalist/ humourist Paul Harvey with that notable Twickenham medium, Madame Vandorcrampon. Together, this fearsome duo have summoned up the shades of clarinettist Henry Lazarus (1815–1895) to review a newly-released album. Since Henry Lazarus was, in addition to being a superb instrumentalist, also, apparently, a caustic critic, we must excuse his fine arrogance.

Colin Bradbury (clarinet), Oliver Davies (piano):
'The Victorian Clarinettist'.
(Discources (All About Music) Ltd., Royal Tunbridge Wells, Kent. ABM 29).

Henry Lazarus (1815–1895): 'Fantasia on Airs from Bellini's 'I Puritani''.
Charles Villiers Stanford (1852-1924): Three Intermezzi, Op 13.
James Waterson (1834–1893): Morceau de Concert.
J. W. Kalliwoda (1800–1866): Morceau de Salon, Op 299.
Donato Lovreglio (1841-1907): Fantasia on Verdi's 'La Traviata'.
Charles Oberthur (1819-1895): Le Desir.

I am moved to commence this dissertation by congratulating Mr Bradbury upon his excellent taste in starting his recital with my own Fantasia; by far the most significant work in his repertoire; a subtle blend of brilliantly effective virtuoso writing and profound musical thoughts. I admire his courage in thus exposing his playing to comparison with my own, and, though he could not hope to surpass me, I am bound to admit that he comes closer than any other aspiring competitor to equalling my artistry. This may be accounted for by the fact that Mr Bradbury was apparently a student of Thurston, who himself studied with one of my own most promising protegés, young Charlie Draper. Sir Arthur Sullivan is indeed fortunate to have secured the services of so distinguished an artist as Mr Bradbury as Professor of Clarinet at the Royal College of Music.

Although the rest of the programme is inevitably something of an anticlimax after my Fantasia, it is nevertheless worthy of comment as a representative selection of the efforts of five of my more distinguished admirers. Charles Stanford is a young composition colleague of mine at the RCM, and wrote these Intermezzi in his earlier days at Cambridge. He often seeks my advice upon writing for the clarinet, and is contemplating a Concerto for the instrument. Recently he has become much influenced by a young German composer, Herr Brahms, who, I understand, has attempted some small pieces for the clarinet. However, I have advised Stanford to look to works of substance, such as my Fantasia, for his inspiration.

James Waterson had the good fortune to study under me at Kneller Hall, and through my bringing his diligence to the notice of the Duke of Cambridge (I frequently take tea with HRH, you know) he secured an appointment as Bandmaster to the Viceroy of India. His clarinet writing retains all the distinguished hallmarks of his early training.

The other side represents three composers who have quite successfully surmounted the crippling handicap of not being British. One must indeed applaud their courage and tenacity in the face of a misfortune of birth which causes most foreigners to give up all efforts to improve themselves and resort to gesticulation and incomprehensible babbling.

The Bohemian, Kalliwoda, has composed several most creditable pieces for the clarinet, of which this Morceau de Salon is perhaps the most attractive. The Italian Lovreglio, although labouring under the additional burden of being a flautist, has written much for the quite competent clarinet players of his country; Signori Carulli, Gambaro, Cavallini and the rest. If only the lira had a more advantageous rate of exchange against the sovereign, it might be within the means of some of these Italian fellows to become really advanced players by studying with me in England. Herr Oberthur has taken such a step by settling in England, and is enjoying the success invariably accorded by the British public to foreign musicians. Indeed, in my all-too-frequent moments of self-denigration, I often wonder if my fame would have been as great had my patronymic been Smith or Brown!

I most earnestly recommend that you purchase this phonograph recording, which should cause you to make every effort to hear Mr Bradbury in person. I am given to understand that he is the incumbent of the principal clarinet position in an ensemble with which I am unfamiliar; the BBC Symphony Orchestra. As more detailed information has not been provided by Mr Harvey, I merely hazard a guess that these cryptic initials may stand for Blackpool Borough Council Symphony Orchestra; presumably one of the worthy little orchestras which enrich the musical life of our many delightful watering places. If this is the case, I am sure that an artist of Mr Bradbury's impressive virtuosity will soon eschew the fatiguing train and hansom cab journey between Blackpool and Kensington, and obtain an appointment at the Queen's Hall, or some equally prestigious London concert rooms, where his fine playing will reach a wider and more enlightened public.

— Henry Lazarus (1815–1895),
2A Neville Terrace, Onslow Gardens,
Kensington

THE DEFFAYET SAXOPHONE QUARTET OF PARIS

As I am constantly saying at LSQ concerts how many saxophone quartets there are on the continent and in the USA, it was gratifying to be able to show people that these foreign quartets are not just a figment of my fevered imagination. This must have been the first visit to these shores of a foreign saxophone quartet since the Quatuor Belge came over some years ago. The personnel of the Quartet is: Soprano: Daniel Deffayet, Professor at the Paris Conservatoire. Alto: Henri-Rene Pollin, Professor at the Rouen Conservatoire. Tenor: Jaques Terry, Principal Saxophone of the Musique de la Garde Republicaine. Baritone: Jean Ledieu, Professor at the Nancy Conservatoire.

At the Washington Hotel a large audience of saxophone enthusiasts heard M. Deffayet start with some alto solos, accompanied at the piano by Alan Hinton. He then changed to soprano to lead the quartet in Marcel Mule transcriptions of pieces by Boccherini, Albeniz and Scarlatti, and two original quartets by Pierre Vellones; *The Dolphins* and *Chromatic Waltz*. After the interval the quartet returned with *Le Petit Conquerant* by Edmond Gaujac and *The Canzona and Variations* from the Glazounov Quartet. They omitted the Schumann Variation (don't we all) but I was a bit disappointed, as I enjoy a cheap trill. (That's an in joke, folks). The finale was Jean Rivier's magnificent *Grave and Presto* (on this occasion Prestissimo!) surely one of the finest pieces of writing in the saxophone quartet repertoire. After much applause they returned for an encore; for a nasty moment I thought they might be going to play to the gallery by doing a horrid bagpipe imitation like that exhibitionistic local quartet; I forget its name. However, I was relieved when M. Deffayet announced, in impeccable French, 'Le Serenade Comique de Jean Francaix.'

RECITAL REVIEW

ELIZABETH ANN FOGLE (clarinet) with PAULA FAN (piano)

Wigmore Hall, London, Saturday November 25th, 1978

Having missed Dr Fogle's previous London recital, I was glad to have this second opportunity, and it was a pleasure to hear once again the fine piano playing of Paula Fan, who seems to be making a speciality of accompanying American clarinettists for London recitals.

Although 4.30 in the afternoon is an unusual time for a recital, its 6.15 finishing time made possible a meaningful assembly of clarinettists in the pub afterwards, without the usual hassle of waiting for opening time, as in the case of earlier afternoon concerts, or worrying about closing time after evening concerts.

Among those present were the two performers, Georgina Dobree, just returned from a most successful lecture-recital tour of the USA. James Schoepflin, of Washington State University, who was passing through London only for the day, after an Austrian tour with the Muhlfeld Trio, and Bill Dakin, an ex-student of David Glazer, now resident in London as legal counsellor to Mobil Oil and official watchdog on reed quality control to the Clarinet and Saxophone Society of Great Britain. (I understand the former appointment to be the more lucrative!)

Many fascinating topics were discussed, such as the behaviour of Dr Fogle's clarinet in the cold and humidity of the Borough of Marylebone as compared with the climate of Arizona. I had to admit that one rarely sees six foot cacti pushing their way up through the pavements of Wigmore Street! The black pull-through with which Dr Fogle swabbed her instrument between each movement had been much admired. It is not, she revealed, a fetish object of some Phoenix swabbing cult, but is black for the very practical reason that she feels it does not show up as much against a black dress when used during orchestral concerts.

EVENTIDE WITH A CLARINET SEXTET

The event, some time ago, at England's Strawberry Hill College started with Mr Doug Ellis welcoming what must have been the largest gathering of clarinettists since the last performance of Havergal Brian's *Gothic Symphony*. Then Ted Planas gave a short talk on the complete clarinet range, including an explanation of the various properties with demonstrations on each by Christopher Gradwell.

Mr Gradwell led us smoothly from the talking into the playing by introducing Thomas Kelly, with whom he played the Poulenc Sonata for B flat and A clarinets. The astringent bitonality of this ebullient work was tastefully understated, as Frank Cordell might (or might not) say. Then it was time to meet the eagerly waited 'Sextour de Clarinettes de Montfraise'; (Strawberry Hill Clarinet Sextet to non-German-speaking readers) which was a fashionably nostalgic exercise d'apres Syd Lawrence, in that it was formed especially to recreate the repertoire of the old Selmer Clarinet Sextet, recorded several decades ago on a couple of 78s which are now collectors' items.

Some of my colleagues who heard about his event via the clarinettists' grapevine thought it was a Clarinet Sextet from France. They must have been brought down not to find them attired in striped jerseys and berets, breathing garlic fumes over the audience! The personnel were, in fact, all well known London players, but I feel it more in keeping with the spirit of the preceedings to introduce them as ... MESSIEURS ... Hale Hambleton *(de l'Opera Nationale)*, E-flat clarinet; Thomas Kelly *(Professeur a l'Ecole Royale de la Musique Militaire)*, first clarinet; Christophe Gradwell *(Professeur au Conservatoire de la Place Mandeville)*, second clarinet; Edouard Planas *Professeur d'Acoustique a la Sorbonne d'Iverbucks)*, alto clarinet; Paul Allen *(des Ballets Fetes)*, bass clarinet; Etienne Trier *(Professeur au Conservatoire de la Rue Prince Consort)*, E-flat contrabass clarinet.

They played Loucheur's *En Famille*, Mozart's *Divertimento No 15,* Bozza's *Luciole* (which turned out to be the same piece as his *Nuages* for saxophone quartet; possibly with extra royalties in mind, as Steve Trier pointed out!), and Mendelssohn's *Rondo Capriccioso*. The playing was as sparkling and professional as one would expect from such a line up. As Wally Horwood sometimes says, one should not single out anyone in such a fine musical team for individual praise, BUT ... I understand that the plague of bats which has infested the Twickenham area is directly attributable to Hale Hambleton's stratospheric E flat playing, while Steve Trier's delicate handling of the mightly wooden E flat contrabass was a revelation to several of us present who regularly emit space monster noises of indeterminate pitch on our B flat contras at CTS, Denham, Olympic and other such alien planets.

The clarinettists then all retired to another room, where a vast quantity of wine and goodies had been appetizingly arranged by Barbara Wigglesworth. All those responsible for the organization of this most enlightening and convivial evening are to be most heartily congratulated on its unqualified success. I trust that we are in for an invigorating round of similar soirees close to the London area.

If any of them want me to organize the Tokyo Saxophone Octet or the Budapest Tarogato Ensemble, they've only to give me a ring, especially if these distinguished Chamber Groups are to be recreated in such a civilized environment at Twickenham. You see, my problem is that I can't afford the bus fare to anywhere further afield, having spent so much money on instruments!

RECORD REVIEW
'BANKERS AT PLAY':
Dixieland by the Nat West Jazz Band

Obtainable from any branch of the National Westminster Bank. Proceeds in aid of the Mental Health Appeal

There has been a most welcome trend lately for large financial corporations such as Banks and Building Societies to subsidise Symphony Concerts and Operatic Productions. For many years large firms, mainly in the North of England, have supported their own Brass Bands. But now the National Westminster Bank is, like, into Jazz, man, with its own eleven piece Dixieland Band, staffed entirely by Bank Managers and other Senior Officials. I've been asked to review their first album, perhaps because they can rely on me for an impartial review, as I've kept my overdraft at Barclays for many years, unlike John Dankworth, who confesses in his sleeve note to having a Nat West account!

The standard of playing is very good; these are obviously the sort of enthusiasts who would be blowing jazz in their spare time, anyway, even if their employers did not support their venture to this extent. The band as a whole has a well rehearsed and disciplined sound, perhaps occasionally a little over contrived for the most all out, raving New Orleans Trad. purist, but, after all, these chaps are wholesome British Bank Managers, not haggard denizens of Basin Street brothels and the like!

The leader is clarinettist Seth Marsh (occasional contributor to CASS News), who composed one of the numbers, *Go Nat West Young Man*, and is featured in *Petite Fleur*. The unusual sound of Steve Davies' C soprano sax contributes interesting solos on several tracks, but the most telling moment, I feel, is where the eleven Bank Managers give a fervent rendering of *Nobody Loves Yuh When Yuh're Down 'n' Out*.

This is an entertaining record, which would be well worth your money if you want to help a good cause and have a swinging knees-up at the same time. Let's hope it's the forerunner of other albums such as 'The Inland Revenue Clarinet Choir', or 'The Westminster Traffic Wardens' Saxophone Consort'. Believe me, friends, we need as many allies as we can get in the corridors of power in these difficult times.

NEW MUSIC REVIEWS
JOHN NOBLE: 'CATS', a Suite for Clarinet and Piano
(Cramer: 90p)

Perhaps I am particularly susceptible at the moment, because my own black and white cat, Domino, has just been carried off in his prime to the happy mousing grounds in the sky, a victim of feline pneumonia. I may add that I have been a cat lover for longer than I've been a clarinet fanatic, so anything which combines the two interests captures my imagination. I suppose Prokofiev started the cat-clarinet cult in *Peter and the Wolf*, but he certainly made the right choice of instrument.

Anyway, these five little pieces by John Noble are delightful clarinet music, judged just by musical standards. Not at all difficult: Grade V, with an approachable piano part. Each piece is dedicated to a different cat of the composer's acquaintance. First comes 'Allegro Pussicato', describing Oscar's miaow and other characteristics. Then 'Tabbioso' is for Beethoven. My only criticism is in this piece, for an impossible turn over and turn back to sign, which could have been avoided easily by printing pieces 1, 2 and 3 across one sheet and 4 and 5 across the other side. However, the bit you have to turn over for is subtitled 'Moggiore', which makes it all worth while! Thirdly comes the happy cat Mozart's piece: 'Purrdendosi', followed by an excursion to the land of the inscrutable harmonic minor scale, homeland of Pippin, who's piece is called 'Cat Mandu', The last word goes to Sam, a black and white minstrel cat, who dances a hoedown called 'Cotton Pickin' Kittin', the tempo of which is Pusstissimo'.

Well, alright, I suppose I should be reviewing significant additions to the clarinet repertoire, such as Boulhausen's 'Ejaculation 77.7 recurring' for seventeen E flat clarinets and prepared washing machine. (Actually that's in the next issue, I think). But I can't help it if I'm in my second childhood; anyway, I predict that *Cats* will become the piece which all your dear little pupils in schools will want to play, so you may as well get used to the idea. The super cover drawing by Trevor Manship of a clarinet tooting tabby should boost sales too. I really wish I'd thought of it first!

GRONE'S DICTIONARY OF MUSIC

(Misleading Lives of the Great Composers) by Howard Burnham and Dick Butterworth. Published by: Emerson Edition, Windmill Farm, Ampleforth, Yorks, England. Price: £2.95

As Fritz Spiegl says in his foreword to this eccentric tome: 'Being funny about music is extremely difficult nowadays.'

In fact, it's always been impossible to make all the people laugh all the time about anything. One man's belly laugh is another man's emetic, as Nietzsche might have said if he'd had Mr Spiegl's command of English. Grone's Dictionary relies heavily on puns and word play. Much of the 'information' offered about composers takes on the character of the occasional inspired misprint in programme notes which one cherishes and shows to one's friends. It also utilises the schoolboy howler style of the 'Bach had nineteen children and practised on a spinster in the attic' variety.

Incidentally, I was disappointed to find no reference to my favourite composer, P. D. Q. Bach. As treasurer of the Twickenham branch of the P. D. Q. Bach Appreciation Society, and principal castrato of the P. D. Q. Bach Choir (for which organisation I have voluntarily given my services) I feel it my duty to protest at this omission on behalf of our founder, Professor Schickele of the University of Southern North Dakota at Hoople.

Serious-minded teachers of musical history may be affronted at the perversion of the facts which their pupils have to remember for examinations, and there may even be a few diehard reactionaries about who do not believe that Dame Ethel Smyth was Sir Edward Elgar in drag! Apart from a handful of extremists such as these, however, most musicians will find much to chuckle over, but I imagine most of the humour would be hard to grasp for someone without a basic grounding in 'conventional' musical history.

Fifty per cent of the book consists of the artwork, which is brilliant, in the Salvador Dali/Heath Robinson/Monty Python school. At its comparatively modest price, it would make a good gift for jaded musicologists and world-weary music critics.

THE CLARINET TEACHER'S COMPANION by Pamela Weston

(Robert Hale & Co. £2.00)

Owing to the greatly increased demand for clarinet teachers in school which has developed over the last decade, many more students now take a teacher's diploma, which invariably includes a paper on 'The Principles of Teaching'. How does one prepare them for this, bearing in mind that they have rarely had much teaching experience at this stage? My own approach is to have my students give me lessons in which I assume the character of an indescribably awful pupil who has every conceivable fault. Over the years I have perfected this role to such a degree that I now have great difficulty in playing properly, but that's my problem! I also give them a list of books to read: Rendall, Kroll, Thurston, Stubbins, etc., yet I always have the uneasy feeling that these profound works are not going to help them much when confronted by their first twelve-year-old gangster with buckteeth and double-jointed fingers, whose ultimate musical ambition is to render 'Stranger on the Shore', a quarter tone flat!

This book will be invaluable, not only to student teachers, but also to experienced players and teachers, who will certainly find some stimulating ideas and new angles on old problems. I only wish it had been available when I first started teaching. If so, I might have been able to give more comfort to the young lady student who said to me, on the eve of an exam, 'Every time I put the clarinet in my mouth I feel as if I'm going to throw up!' I experienced a sense of inadequacy as I replied heartily, 'Never mind, dear, I've had that feeling every Monday morning for the last twenty-five years!'

CLARINET VIRTUOSI OF THE PAST
by Pamela Weston

Most books on the clarinet and its history are mainly concerned with the technical development of the instrument, its acoustical properties and other such weighty matters. Admirable and necessary as these books are, and I assure you I've read every one of them dutifully, I must admit that, being a mechanical moron and a scientific ignoramus, I invariably turn to those sections which deal, albeit sketchily, with the lives of flesh and blood clarinettists. Being one myself, I suppose I identify with them.

Imagine my joy when this book came out, devoted entirely to my favourite people. As I now re-read it for the third time, I have a distinct impression that it was written especially for me! That's why I want to tell *Woodwind World* readers about it so they can share it with me.

Pamela Weston is a noted British clarinettist and teacher, who has spent literally years in painstaking research, and travelled all over Europe in search of material for this book.

We start in 1742, with a 'Mr Charles, the Hungarian' treating Dublin society to a fantastic tour de force on French horn and three instruments 'never heard in this Kingdom before'; the clarinet, the 'hautbois de amour' and the 'shalamo'. (This last one a good 200 years before the John Wayne movie, folks).

We follow the early virtuosi on their prodigious tours of Europe; Beer, Tausch, Crusell, Hermstedt, Blaes and the rest, endlesssly crisscrossing each other's tracks in springless, unheated carriages between Paris, Vienna, Prague, Budapest, St Petersburg.

A full chapter is devoted to each of the three composer-player relationships which formed the backbone of the clarinet repertoire; Mozart-Stadler, Weber-Baermann and Brahms-Muhlfeld.

Three chapters placed at chronological intervals through the book return to Paris to trace the technical advances in clarinet design made by Lefevre, Muller and Klose.

I have always been fascinated by Henry Lazarus, who dominated the English clarinet scene for the latter half of the 19th century. At Kneller Hall there is a photograph of the Professors in 1859, posing at a spot which I pass every morning. In the centre is Lazarus, bewhiskered, frock-coated, top hat in hand, smug in the knowledge that he is being paid seven shillings per hour for his sevices, while on his left a humbler personage, one Thomas Sullivan, receives only three shillings and and sixpence per hour. (Don't worry, Tom; one day your little boy, Arthur, will be a Knight of the Realm, Director of the Royal College of Music and Britain's leading composer!) Anyway, Miss Weston's book has given me much intriguing information about Lazarus, concluding with the fact that, when he died in 1895, his effects totalled £1,400, and were administered by his illegitimate son.

I found the account of the death of another English player, George Clinton, in 1913, somewhat disturbing. It seems he dropped dead in a train en route from Trinity College of Music to Kneller Hall. These are the two establishments at which I teach. Miss Weston says he overstrained his heart. I think I'll just go and lie down for a bit.

The book has some fascinating illustrations, ranging from manuscripts of early Concerti, portraits of most of the players, their instruments, and some particularly interesting pictures of Brahms and Muhlfeld which Miss Weston obtained personally from the Muhlfeld family. It concludes with the death, in 1953, of Frederick Thurston, with whom Miss Weston and myself both studied.

To say I recommend this book would be an understatement. I'd like to write a lot more about it, but won't as I want to start reading it again, right now!

MORE CLARINET VIRTUOSI OF THE PAST by Pamela Weston

The discriminating movie-goer views sequels with suspicion, often justifiably so. 'Son of Lassie meets Frankenstein's Daughter at the OK Corrall' is a sure-fire non-starter to achieve the quality of its progenitors. Yet Pamela Weston, motivated by the worldwide response of clarinettists to their very own history book, 'Clarinet Virtuosi of the Past', has defied this prejudice to give us a companion volume.

The original dealt with the lives of the giants of the clarinet in great detail, and was written in narrative style. 'More Virtuosi' has a different format; its main section is a biographical reference book containing alphabetical entries for almost 1,000 clarinettists, including those already dealt with more fully in Volume 1. Yet this is no dry 'Who was Who in Court Circles'. Characters, tragedies and epic adventures emerge from the succinctly drawn thumbnail sketches. The hard-necked charlatan, Schalk, who was 'a disgrace to the breed of basset horn players'. Pollard of the Coldstream Guards and Halle Orchestra, who 'went insane and hanged himself in the wash-house on April 7th, 1866 aged only 33'.

The German Eisert, captured with a French Military Band in the Peninsular War, brought to England and eventually made 1st clarinet of his captors' Court Orchestra. These random examples could respectively form the basis of comic, tragic or adventure novels. These are 32 pages of portraits and photographs to complement this section.

The second part of the book is a list of places and the notable clarinettists who held appointments there. Would you like to know who succeeded Demnitz in the Court orchestra at Mecklenburg-Schwerill? Or who taught at the Madrid Conservatoire in 1829? Here you will find the answers.

The final section is a list of all the compositions mentioned in both volumes, with performers and dates. Where can I get a copy of Schalk's basset horn solo 'Reminiscences of Switzerland (with Echo effects)'? Nobody's played it since 1834, and I feel the world deserves another Schalk! All the people in the first book were such GOOD players, but I can identify with poor, defiant Schalk, soldiering on in the face of terrible reviews, one of which provides my favourite quote: 'The delicate tone of his instrument does not go well with his moustache.' I expect he had dandruff and halitosis as well!

No praise is too high for Miss Weston's consummate scholarship and painstaking research, so don't delay; order your copy now. Put it in your bookshelf next to 'Clarinet Virtuosi of the Past' and you will be the lucky possessor of the greatest double volume in the entire literature of the clarinet.

8 Kneller Hall

It has been suggested that I introduce this chapter by relating how I come to have spent the last twenty years teaching at Kneller Hall. In 1969 I left the Bournemouth Symphony Orchestra and returned to London to freelance once more. One of my first engagements was a 'Friday Night is Music Night' with the BBC Concert Orchestra, on which the guest band was the Irish Guards, still conducted by 'Jiggs' Jaeger, who had been Director of Music when I was a member of the band over a decade before.

We were chatting during the rehearsal, and Jiggs said, 'This is my last engagement with the Irish. I take over as Director of Music of Kneller Hall on Monday.'

'That's funny,' I replied, 'I live near there, in Twickenham.'

The following Monday morning I was having a bath, when the phone rang. Shivering in the hall, dripping wet, I answered it. It was Jiggs.

'Just arrived at Kneller Hall,' he said, 'and I find that two of the old Clarinet Professors have just retired. (George Garside and Henry Pipe). Get over here right away, and see if you'd like to do a bit of teaching for us!'

Well, I did just that, and twenty years later I'm still there! For the first ten years I only taught clarinet, and Pat Dixon was the saxophone Professor. Then it became a Civil Service job, and when Pat retired I was asked to take over the saxophones as well.

I'm now in the venerable position of being the Senior Professor (in length of service, that is). The only official duty which goes with this title is to reply to the Commandant's toast at the Professors' Christmas Luncheon in the Officers' Mess. For this, I always try to think what Henry Lazarus would have said when he was my equivalent over a century ago!

THE TRUMPETERS OF THE ROYAL MILITARY SCHOOL OF MUSIC KNELLER HALL

When I first started teaching the clarinet at Kneller Hall five years ago, I stepped from my car at 8.30am on the first morning, hoping to merge discreetly into the routine. With a pile of music under one arm and my clarinet under the other I kicked the car door shut. As if the click was an eagerly awaited signal to Archangel Gabriel's Director of Music, poised expectantly on a cloud, baton at the ready, the crisp morning air was suddenly rent by a mighty fanfare, resonant with such martial pomp as to make the last trump on the Day of Judgement pale into an insignificant toot on the recorder.

As I sprawled, shocked and dazed, across the bonnet of my car, pages of clarinet studies, concertos, sonatas scattering to the four winds, I realised that I was hearing the legendary Kneller Hall Trumpeters. 'It's nice to be made welcome at a new job,' I thought, 'but they really shouldn't have gone to so much trouble just to mark my arrival, and so early in the morning too.' I regained my composure, collected up my music, and commenced a dignified progress to my teaching room, giving a casual wave in the trumpeters' direction. 'Thank you, gentlemen, and a very good morning to you, too!' I shouted. But they heard not a word as they were launched already into another flourish which made the first seem a distant echo of muted violins.

Inside my room, my first pupil, a gangling Glaswegian, with pimples and a terrible cold, was keening miserably up and down a strange Oriental scale of his own invention. It had a flattened supertonic and a sharpened subdominant. I later discovered that he imagined it to be a harmonic minor scale, and always started playing it when he observed me approaching, hoping to convey the impression of being immersed in constructive practice.

'Do they often go off like that?' I asked.

'Who, surr?' he replied, furtively pushing a dog-end into the top of his boot.

'Why, those trumpeters out there.'

'Och, eye, evra bordig, blawid thr'wee heids awf.'

I still play the Fanfare Game, as I find it a beneficial ego therapy. It requires split-second timing as I drive slowly into the grounds, watching the trumpeters forming up.

I dawdle over switching off the engine for a few moments, and get out of my car just as the Bandmaster raises his baton. 'Clunk,

Trumpeters of the Royal Military School of Music.

click' has nothing on 'Clunk, tara... tatataratara... tara, etc., etc.' It's just the thing to make one feel important on a Monday morning.

The Kneller Hall fanfare team is virtually a full brass section of B flat trumpets, tenor trombones and G bass trombones, all in elongated form with valves. Although Kneller Hall had provided teams of trumpets for state occasions since the mid-nineteenth century, these chromatic fanfare instruments were introduced by Lieut. H. E. Adkins, who was Director of Music in the 1920s, the original set being made to his own specifications. At first the E flat soprano trumpet was also employed, but this has now been dispensed with.

The usual disposition of parts is: three or four trumpets, two tenor trombones and one bass trombone. The total number of players depends on the type of engagement, which could be anything from a Royal Wedding in Westminster Abbey to the 'Miss Pontin' Competition at the Albert Hall. The minimum team consists of eight players: two 1st trumpets, one 2nd, one 3rd, one 1st trombone, one 2nd trombone and two bass trombones. This line up is expanded in proportion up to the maximum team of twenty-four players, which is employed to open the Kneller Hall Wednesday evening Summer Concerts. Varying amounts of percussion, from a pair of timpani to a full battery, may be added, according to the taste of the composer. Most of the players are Student Bandmasters, but a few of the best brass pupils may be used to make up the numbers.

It's always good to end on a controversial note. Being a rather timid and retiring woodwind player, I do not usually go out of my way to join in brass players' arguments; we have enough in the woodwind family. However, I mention, for what it's worth, that I have heard some purists say that they prefer the thinner, medieval sound of natural trumpets, as employed by the State Trumpeters of the Household Cavalry. I remember being very surprised to hear what natural trumpets actually sound like, after being brought up on Hollywood historical epics where two heralds, wearing emblazoned tabards and gold chainmail cod-pieces, mount the battlements with eight-feet-long natural trumpets, and on the command 'Beholde, ye Kinge cometh!' give us two stereophonic minutes of the MGM Studio Orchestra brass section.

The best argument in favour of the wider-bore, chromatic instruments is this list of fanfares, most of them written especially for the Kneller Hall Trumpeters. All these notable composers would not have produced such an impressive and varied array of triumphant flourishes if they had been restricted to the natural harmonic series.

THE CLARINET CHOIR

... or what America does today, Kneller Hall will be doing next Friday morning

What is wrong with British military bands? I am sure that every reader has his own pet hobby-horse to answer that one, but since I've been given the opportunity I'm going to hop around on mine for a while.

My answer is this; they have no basic tone colour running from top to bottom of the compass.

The symphony orchestra has its violins, violas, cellos and double basses, and what we have is clarinets; in which case the British military band is like an orchestra with lots of violins, no violas or double basses and perhaps one solitary cellist, unhappily scratching away at a tenor saxophone part.

This is a great pity, because the full clarinet family is the only homogeneous group of wind instruments which covers the range of the string family. Yet we are utilising only the top 40 per cent of it.

So I have formed all my pupils into The Kneller Hall Clarinet Choir, in an effort to show what can be done with a full clarinet family.

SEPARATE ENTITY

The clarinet choir should be the exact equivalent of the orchestra's strings; the basic tone colour throughout the band's compass, and also capable of performing as a complete and separate entity, just as a string orchestra does.

The standard clarinet choir is basically a seven-part combination; E flats, 1st, 2nd and 3rd, B flats, E flat altos, B flat basses and B flat contrabass clarinets. Many of the American scores we use also include parts for A flat sopranino and E flat contrabass, but these are always optional.

Exact proportion of balance between the parts is, of necessity, dictated by the availability of the larger instruments. The American *ideal* is: two E flats, four 1sts, four 2nds, four 3rds, four altos, four basses and two contrabasses.

Yes, yes. I can hear the hoots of laughter at the thought of indenting for that lot! I have a wistful chuckle myself when I read it in the scores. However, don't be discouraged; that's an ideal, remember.

Our clarinet choir at Kneller Hall is very top heavy. But it works.

As you can imagine, the school's resources consist of E flats, B flats, and one bass clarinet. To these I have added, from my own stockpile of instruments, accumulated painfully one by one on hire purchase over twenty fanatical years — one E flat alto, one basset horn (tenor clarinet in F, used as an extra alto by writing out all the parts down a tone), one bass and one contrabass.

But, you may ask, how do the pupils who are, after all, the most important people at Kneller Hall, benefit from this exercise?

WHAT BENEFIT?

I assign the lower instruments to the best players, and they feel more fulfilled by having responsible, independent parts to play on their own. Also, I think they appreciate the fact that I have enough confidence in them to let them use about £1,500-worth of my own instruments. I admit that, at first, I used to hover about like an anxious mother hen as they put them together, but nowadays I feel confident that my chicks are in careful hands.

My idea is to try to leave enough strong players on B flat to have one as leader of each section, each of whom gains confidence from this responsibility. The others benefit from hearing themselves without the usual all-pervading blanket of brass in the backs of their necks.

I use all the E flat pupils, which is generally too many but, of course, they need the experience. The ideal would be two very experienced players only.

MY RESPONSIBILITY

The E flat teaching at Kneller Hall is solely my responsibility, and I am becoming more and more convinced that nobody should be allowed to so much as open the lid on an E flat case until he has had at least two years on B flat — then only the best of players. To make a lad learn fingerings and counting rhythms on E flat is like sending a learner driver along Oxford Street in a Grand Prix racing car for a bit of practice; lethal to himself and other road-users!

To be a successful E flat player you need a lip of iron, nerves of steel and an ear like a bat — bat, I said, not boot.

However, I am digressing from the subject of the clarinet choir. What can the average Bandmaster hope to do in this direction, and what would be the benefits to his band?

I know that several already use a bass clarinet, and this is a step in the right direction. In the profession, nearly every clarinettist *must* have a bass as part of his standard equipment nowadays, so there are quite a few reasonably priced second-hand ones about if one keeps a look out for them.

But please do not waste your bass clarinet on playing tenor sax parts, which don't use the bottom, and best, fifth of the instrument. If there is no proper part available for it, write one. It won't take long.

Alto and contrabass clarinets are now being manufactured n large quantities in the United States for the schools market, and some are gradually finding their way to Britain. The price of a contrabass is about the same as a good baritone sax, and I'll bet you managed to afford one of those for the dance band.

The only situation where you full clarinet choir would not be of much use is in the marching band, but as all your alto, bass and contrabass players would be primarily B flat players, they would just revert to B flat for parades. There is no doubling problem, as the alto, bass and contrabass parts are all written in treble clef, and the fingering is identical to that of the B flat.

CHURCH SERVICES

Your clarinet choir would really come into its own at church services. Imagine the sonority of a Bach Chorale played by the full family in a nice resonant church!

In the band concert situation the overall tone-colour of your complete band would be greatly enhanced, while the clarinet choir could perform the occasional separate item, giving the brass and percussion a rest and providing the audience with a change of sound.

I think you will find that all this will happen here eventually; like it or not, we usually follow America after a few years, don't we? Hot dogs, Coca-Cola, Stabrite buttons, bass guitars, clarinet choirs . . . what's the difference?

The argument that the British Army managed very nicely, thank you, with just E flats and B flats for a very long time does not discourage me. After all, the British Army managed very nicely, thank you, at the Battle of Agincourt, using longbows; yet now even my poor old Lee-Enfield rifle, which I used to polish lovingly at the Guards' Depot, has long been obsolete.

End of sermon. A silver collection will be taken as you leave. Please give generously. Proceeds go towards my 'Buy a contrabass clarinet for a British soldier' fund. Thank you.

Contrabass, basses and alto clarinets of the Kneller Hall Clarinet Choir.

The Kneller Hall Clarinet Choir (1976) — the soloist is John Harle, leader of the Myrha Saxophone Quartet and distinguished saxophone recitalist.

Soloist Tony Spencer — dedicatee of 'Improvisation on a Martial Inversion'.

The Kneller Hall Clarinet Choir.

l to r: Paul Harvey, Gordon Jacob and Pat Dixon (professor of Saxophone at the time).

PROFS. HARTMANN	ZEISS	SNELLING	MANDEL	MARTIN	MANN
Flute	Cornet and Trumpet	Bassoon	Director of Music	Clarinet	French Horn
HUGHES	PHASEY	LAZARUS	BARRETT	SULLIVAN	COLE
Ophicleide	Euphonium	Clarinet	Oboe	Bombardon	School Master

Top: Kneller Hall professors, 1859; and below: in the same spot over a century later.

9 World Saxophone Congress

The World Saxophone Congress was started by Paul Brodie of Toronto and Eugene Rousseau of Indiana University, at the 1969 Northwestern Band Conference in Chicago. This was repeated in Chicago the following year, but the first truly International WSC was the third, held in Toronto in 1972, organised mainly by the same team, with the addition of James Houlik, of East Carolina.

In 1974 the WSC first came to Europe, at the instigation of Jean-Marie Londeix, of Bordeaux. It was while participating in this WSC that the London Saxophone Quartet was invited to organise the Fifth Congress in London in 1976.

Over the course of these four years, 1972–76, I wrote so many words about the WSC that just typing this page is bringing me out in a cold sweat of deja vu! If you want more details about the WSCs in which we participated you'll have to make do with reading the various articles in this chapter which I wrote at the time.

After organizing the 1976 WSC we'd all had enough, and didn't attend any more. I switched my allegiance to the International Clarinet Society, performing at the 1984 Convention in London, and the 1986 one at the University of Washington, in Seattle.

THIRD WORLD SAXOPHONE CONGRESS

DAY 1:   Friday, August 18, 1972, 9am
In the recital hall of the Edward Johnston building, International Coordinator James Houlik officially opened the Congress. The first day was a survey of Canada's saxophone talent, assembled by our host, Torontonian virtuoso Paul Brodie.

DAY 2: Saturday, August 19, 9am
The International section of the Congress gets under way; and how! The New York Quartet; Ray Beckenstein, Al Regni, Dave Tofani and Danny Bank. This is the group which has everything, kids; an attack like a fist in the gut; intonation that would satisfy Boulez; all the technique in the world and a range of dynamics from the caress of a butterfly's wing to a Jumbo jet taking off from Kennedy! All this is put across with such relaxed professionalism that you would think they were just warming up for a recording session. And this was at 9 in the morning, don't forget; before your average saxophonist has even groped under the bed for his horn to blow his first bottom B flat of the day. If I ever get to hear them at 9pm I guess I may go take up penguin breeding in Tierra Del Fuego!

DAY 3: Sunday, August 20, 12.30pm
Perhaps the most eagerly awaited moment of the Congress now followed. Jean-Marie Londeix gave the Premiere of Guy Lacour's *Hommage a Jaques Ibert*. The work seems to me traditional French virtuoso writing at its best. Of course it was supremely effective on this occasion; to make a dispassionate pronouncement on the quality of the work, I would have to hear it played by somebody other than Londeix. As far as I'm concerned, le Maitre could stand on a concert platform for three hours playing Scales and Arpeggios, and my jaw would be handing in my lap all the time.

In the evening, Le Quatuor Belge appeared, led by Francois Daneels. They showed us quartet playing at its most polished; the effect was like an enormous saxophone keyboard, played by one brilliant and sensitive pianist. The moto perpetuo variation of the Pierre-Max Dubois was executed with such beautifully controlled panache that it moved the audience to spontaneous applause.

Finally we viewed a short Belgian film on the life of Adolphe Sax, which M. Daneels had brought with him. It is an admirable, well made little film as far as it goes, but is not long enough to do more than whet the appetite. It seems to be designed more to arouse the interest of young non-saxophonists, rather than we obsessive professionals, and will probably succeed in that. I hope some Hollywood Producer may see it, and be moved to give us something on a more epic scale. How about *The Life and Loves of Adolphe Sax*, starring George C. Scott in the title role, with Elizabeth Taylor as Augusta Holmes, Raquel Welch as Clara Schumann and special guest appearance of Frank Sinatra as Berlioz?

DAY 4: Monday, August 21, 9am
The morning was brought to a spectacular close by Harvey Pittel of Los Angeles.

His first piece, a soprano solo by Emmett Yoshioka; was the most beautiful piece of music I heard at the Congress. Then a Halsey Stevens alto solo, also a fine piece of writing, was brilliantly played. For his Finale Harvey gave us a 'sound event', the mere description of which would normally have had me out of my seat and heading for the nearest bar before you could say 'Karl-Heinz Stockhausen, ring modulator'. Yet, on this occasion, the sheer force of Harvey's personality kept me at my post, like a small furry animal hypnotised by a snake! It seems he had pre-recorded several tracks on tape, and, with the aid of a click-track can on one ear, was going to play with himself. He had previously issued the audience with duplicated sheets describing the finer points of what we were to hear, and enumerating the revolutionary effects we were about to witness, such as key rattling, ring tapping, foot scraping (both back and forth AND circular), burping down the instrument (a few pints of beer is the best preparation for this technique; I've been doing it for years!) and vocal grunting (like, I was shouting 'OOH!' in Latin-American dance bands twenty years ago, man). When Harvey was finally equipped for this extravaganza he reminded me of a cross between Roland Kirk, as I first saw him at the Five Spot in Greenwich Village, festooned with an entire sax section and other paraphernalia, and a cleancut All-American astronaut, moonwards bound. He had one assistant working the tape recorders and another (whom I gathered had been specially trained for the job as West Point Military Academy) standing by with an armful of saxophones, ready to hand them to Harvey for quick changes. What's that you say? . . . The work? Oh yes, he did play it, eventually, but it was an anti-climax after that build up! If ever I write a work for solo saxophone, I would rather Harvey Pittel premiered it than anyone else, as he would get the last ounce of effect from any piece, however dull. I must make sure he gets a playing and acting part in my hypothetical Adolphe Sax film; he'd go over big with Liz and Raquel.

After lunch George Wolfe, Indiana U. and then . . . Great Heavens! The London Saxophone Quartet! . . . That's us! . . . Hale, Chris and Dave crouch, huddled together in a corner of the bandroom, whimpering pitifully; claw-like fingers twitching furtively at their return air tickets. . . . It's a Big Whip Job. . . . 'Get out there and enjoy yourselves, you bums!' I scream, and we shuffle towards the gate of the arena, chanting, 'We are enjoying ourselves. . . . we are enjoying ourselves,' over and over again. Out there, around the blood soaked sand, five hundred saxophonist Caesars sit with heavy lidded, beady eyes fixed on the four chairs in the centre, thumbs twitching impatiently in the midway position.

I don't remember much about our concert, except that we really did enjoy ourselves. I seemed to hear clapping and cheering, but perhaps that was for the four girls we hired from the Bloor Street Burlesk House to hold our music, wearing just a sax sling and two soprano reeds each. (Well, baritone reeds are so expensive).

Anyway, I'm very glad to report that many people came up to me afterwards clamouring for parts of the new British works by Richard Stoker, John Rushby-Smith, William Sweeny, Carey Blyton, Martin Jones and myself which we had played. It seemed they had enjoyed the serious, contemporary works we had selected, which treat the saxophone as a melodic, not a percussion instrument, and appreciated the touches of humour I deliberately incorporate into my own pieces to leaven the pomposity of so much modern writing.

Well, a few cold beers slid down between four pulsating embouchures with no trouble at all, and we returned for the final concert, which was to be broadcast by CBC, Jean-Marie Londeix came on first, played three Koechlin Etudes superlatively, and then repeated the Lacour *Hommage a Ibert*. I had no sooner got my jaw hitched up from my lap again, when on came Eugene Rousseau to play a Sonata by Violet Archer, a CBC commission. It seemed to me a sincere attempt to produce some meaningful music for saxophone, but was spoilt by a pseudo-bluesy slow movement. I find this distressing on two counts: one, why do composers, commissioned to write a saxophone work, feel obliged to put in a 'jazzy bit', and two, why do straight composers ever expose themselves to ridicule by attempting to write aforesaid 'jazzy bits' unless they are steeped in jazz like Bernstein or Previn? It takes a jazzman to write effective jazz, and the efforts of most straight composers sound like a 1920 edition of *Guide to Busking*.

For the grand finale of the WSC a large string orchestra filled the stage, to perform a Divertimento for Alto Saxophone and Strings, with Paul Brodie as soloist, conducted by the composer, a distinguished local academic, from whom the work had been commissioned by the WSC. Admirable as this gentleman's academic reputation may be, I can only assume that either he loathes the saxophone, or hates avant-garde music so much that he decided to write a piece parodying all the nastiest facets of this particular form of show-biz. Paul Brodie did what was asked of him with considerable aplomb, and managed to convey the impression that he was involved with the goings on, as I shall be doing in Stockhausen's latest epic at the BBC in London next week. What else can we do? The string players' faces gave the game away as they rattled, banged and slapped at all the hackneyed old 'avant-garde' string effects which you can hear any day of the week in London, (or at the University of Oshkosh, Winconsin) if you get your kicks from seeing a Stradivarius disintegrating into firewood. One of the Toronto critics said that this was 'the most imaginative piece of the evening'. Now, some of the things I can imagine being done with a saxophone would make your hair curl, but I wouldn't write them into a piece of music, because I love the saxophone as a medium of musical expression, not a cheap gimmick machine. After the concert I had a terrible nightmare in which Jean-Marie Londeix came on in drag, and played *Laffin' Sax*, and I was jumping up, shouting, 'Non, non, arrettez-vouz, Maitre, ce n'est pas votre metier!' But there were lots of music critics there shouting, 'Yeah, man, what a freaky happening; dig that groovy sound-event!' Pierre Boulez came, in, dressed as a New York cop, and dragged me out of the theatre, as Londeix went into a soft-shoe shuffle routine while eating his saxophone, which was made of candy. I shouted, 'Sales cochons; qu'est ce qu'avez vous fait au premier maitre du saxophone?' But Patrolman O'Boulez started hitting me on the head with his nightstick and I woke up in bed with my wife hitting me on the head with a pillow. 'Why are you screaming obscenities in bad French at three o'clock in the morning?' she asked. 'Must be the cold beer and pizza,' I mumbled.

Well, to sum up. The saxophone is alive and well, and living in Belgium, France, the USA, Canada, Japan and quite a few other places, even Great Britain. The players are in excellent shape, too, and are reproducing extensively. The people I worry about are the composers. The musical public are not going to take the saxophone seriously now, if they hear it wailing and rattling its keys and doing nanny-goat vibrato, any more than they did when they heard exactly the same noises in 1920.

How, then, can a composer extend the saxophone's possibilities? Upwards, certainly; the more we have to play in the altissimo register, the better we'll become at it. Forget the old obsession with the alto, and write more for soprano, tenor and baritone. Multiphonics? Certainly worth experimenting with, though I am tempted to paraphrase Dr Johnson's remark about the dog walking on its hind legs; 'One applauds, not because it does it well, but because it does it at all.' As for the other 'effects', consign them to the dustbin, along with *Laffin' Sax* and the rest. Paul Brodie once said, 'The saxophone is something to sing through.' So, composers, write for the saxophone as if it were a gorgeous opera singer, who is also a virtuoso on flute, oboe and trumpet, and you won't go far wrong.

Sorry if some of this sounds a bit crabby, but I wrote it on a Greyhound bus going from Toronto to New York and back, and the air conditioning wasn't working too well.

We had a marvellous time at the World Saxophone Congress, and made a lot of new friends. Congratulations to Paul Brodie, Jim Houlik and all the other organisers for a wonderful four days in Toronto. 'VIVE LE SAXOPHONE', BUT LET US NOT STAND IDLY BY WHILE, UNDER THE GUISE OF EMANCIPATION, IT MERELY EXCHANGES ONE FORM OF MUSICAL EXPLOITATION FOR ANOTHER.

COME HOME, LAFFIN' SAX, ALL IS FORGIVEN
A bitter epilogue to the World Saxophone Congress

I leaned back in my seat on the jumbo jet, unfastened my safety belt and plugged in my two dollar earphones. The fact that the first thing I heard was my three London Saxophone Quartet colleagues playing in 'Rhapsody in Blue' with the London Symphony Orchestra was only a momentary setback to my contentment. Pausing only to castigate Gershwin for not writing a soprano part, I switched to another channel. On this one Norman Barker, a member of the Krein Saxophone Quartet, was playing a smoochy alto solo with Mantovani's orchestra. With a resigned sigh, I removed my earphones, and, stuffing myself with roast chicken while thinking noble thoughts about what I could do to carry on with the great work of improving the saxophone's image, waited for the movie to start. This was to be a French gangster movie, but my nagging fear that the hero would turn out to be a pupil of Marcel Mule, who robbed banks in order to buy a platinum saxophone, proved to be groundless.

Next day, having arrived home without incident, but still drowsy from the five hours time difference, I threw my alto into the car and proceeded to Maida Vale BBC Studios, where the first rehearsal for a Prom. Concert for which I had been engaged was taking place. Chris Gradwell was playing tenor with me, and I was very pleased that my first date back in London after attending the WSC was on saxophone, as I felt that, now I had heard most of the best players in the world at first hand, I had the right sounds in my head at last, and the BBC Symphony Orchestra were really in for a treat. The concert was to be all American music, conducted by Harold Faberman. 'Aha,' I thought, 'as this chap's an American, he will really appreciate some fine saxophone playing.'

I arrived at the studio and warmed up, trying hard to sound like a combination of Londeix, Sinta, Pittel, Brodie and Rousseau. I was playing in a piece by Virgil Thompson, and I noticed the magic four-letter word, SOLO, drawing near. 'Here we go,' I thought, 'get a load of what a serious saxophonist, who's just been to the WSC sounds like.' What's this? The stick is tapping the rostrum; perhaps he's going to ask the strings to play softer, so he can more fully enjoy the beautiful purity of my alto sound. 'Hey, sax,' says the stick. 'Are you addressing me, sir?' 'Yeah, like, I mean, it don't sound like a sax, y'know? Like, er, yak it up more; wide vib; short dotted eighth notes; gimme all that 1920 jazz, y'know what I mean?'

No, no, it can't be true; not today, of all days! It must be one of those awful nightmares I get: like where I'm doing comedy night on the pier at Bridlington, wearing a false red nose, and playing *Laffin' Sax*, like I used to when I was about sixteen and Jim Houlik is in the audience, and he says, 'I would like you to come and play that at the WSC' and I'm sitting on a plane, still wearing my false nose, and then I'm on the stage at the WSC, playing *Laffin' Sax*, and Jim is saying, 'I brought this fellow over as a warning to you all, how not to play the saxophone,' and everyone is booing and throwing tomatoes, and I wake up, sweating profusely.

But no; it's for real; and what would you do? Being a well known mercenary hypocrite, from way back, I play it the way the stick wants it! 'Yeah, yeah,' shouts the stick, 'that's a great sound, man; gimme more, gimme more!'

I am writing to ask if I should turn in my WSC badge now, or wait until the next Congress, when I can be formally drummed out, by having all my reeds broken and my sling cut, to the accompaniment of all the members trilling on bottom B flat to B natural.

It should make quite an impressive ceremony; please let me know if you would like me to write special music for it.

THE FOURTH WORLD SAXOPHONE CONGRESS

This summer the World Saxophone Congress left the North American Continent for the first time, to be held in Bordeaux. The host and principal organiser was Jean-Marie Londeix, Professor of Saxophone at Bordeaux Conservatoire and the author of a great deal of teaching material, including the standard reference book on saxophone repertoire, *125 Years of Music for Saxophone*. The suburb of Talence is the location of the huge campus of the University of Bordeaux, of which the Congress took over a large theatre, two smaller halls and a complete dormitory village. There were over five hundred participants from many different countries, including France, Belgium, USA, England, Canada, Austria, Denmark, Holland, Norway, Poland, Russia and Japan.

The Congress was officially opened by the founder and Grand Master of the French school of saxophone playing, Marcel Mule, who is now enjoying a well-earned retirement and looks more like a man of 50 than his actual age of 73. The opening concert was given by students of the Bordeaux Conservatoire, dressed in the costume of Adolphe Sax's period, playing ensemble music written soon after his invention of the instrument: Sextuor (1850) by Georges Kastner, *Sigisbée* (1848) by Emile Jonas, and *Honneur à Sax* (1850) by Jean-Nicolas Savari.

After lunch, we (the LSQ, that is) participated in a 'concert of Four Nations', consisting of a very interesting new work entitled *Score*, by American composer George Heussenstam. The resources employed are four saxophone quartets and four percussion players; each quartet, with its own percussionist, being stationed in a different corner of the hall, with the conductor in the middle.

The four nations represented were France (Ensemble de Saxophones Français), Canada (Quebec Quartet), USA (New York Quartet) and England (LSQ).

In the evening, the venue moved to the *Jardin Public*, for a concert of American music for solo saxophone and Concert Band, played by several leading American soloists with the Musique Municipale de Bordeaux.

The second morning was notable for a tour de force by Robert Black, in which he led a recital by the Northwestern University Quartet on soprano, and immediately re-appeared with his alto to give a triumphant solo performance. The evening concert took the form of a 'Soiree Belge', in which we heard the Belgian Quartet, the Brussells Quartet, several Belgian soloists, and a delightful finale by the 'Septuor de Saxophones de Bruxelles', directed by François Daneels. This is a prodigious 'one of each' combination: sopranino, soprano, alto, tenor, baritone, bass and contrabass. As soon as I saw three perspiring Belgians dragging the formidable contrabass onto the stage, I knew my life's work would not be complete until I had formed my own 'Septuor de Saxophones de Twickenham'! Auditions will be held shortly for contrabass saxophone players living in the Middlesex area.

On the third morning an early reveille was necessary for the English contingent to support a 9am recital by John Denman, co-principal clarinet at Sadlers Wells Opera. His programme consisted of new British works for alto and piano, including a Rhapsodia by the versatile scientist-singer-composer-pianist, Eric 'Spike' Hughes, who made the Channel crossing especially to act as John's accompanist. We had to spend the rest of the morning on a final rehearsal for our afternoon concert, so, unfortunately missed the foremost exponents of the Japanese school, which now boasts a remarkable array of fine players, headed by the venerable Aarata Sakaguchi, who, I gather, taught most of them himself.

Our programme consisted of new British quartets by Gordon Jacob, Frank Cordell, Carey Blyton, James Patten, Geoffrey Grey and the bizarre 'enfant terrible' of the East Twickenham school of composition, Paul Harvey. He had produced a dreadful work for the occasion called *A Saxophonist's Nightmare*, or *The Worst Piece Ever Written for Saxophone Quartet*. I was unfortunate enough to obtain an exclusive interview with the composer in which he stated: 'I feel that, with this work, I have at last achieved my lifelong ambition to become a third rate composer.' When asked to elucidate, he added, 'First rate composers suffer a lot, because they think nobody appreciates their work fully. Second rate composers also suffer because they want to be considered first rate composers. Third rate composers have all the fun, because they don't care what anybody thinks of their music.'

The London Saxophone Quartet (Paul Harvey, Hale Hambleton, Christopher Gradwell and David Lawrence) rehearsing at the University of Toronto, Canada.

Marcel Mule talking with the author 1976.

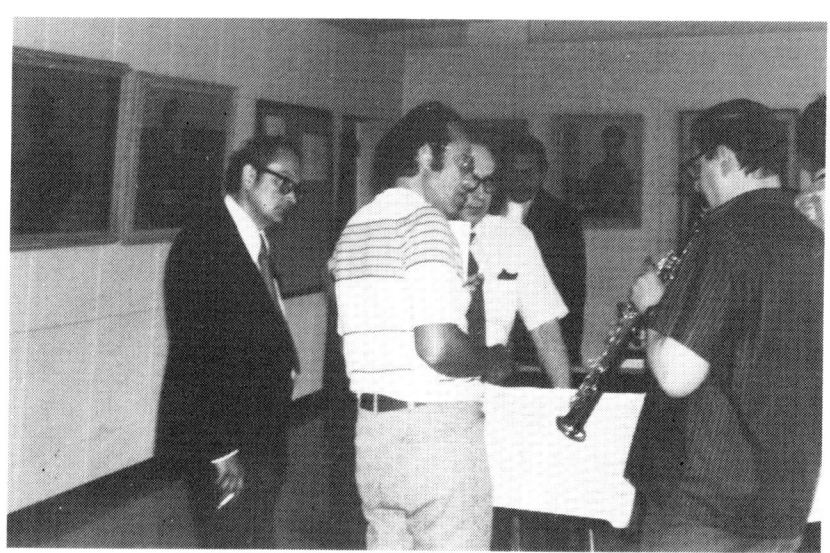

Paul Harvey playing his Concertino for soprano saxophone, Royal College of Music, 1976.

The author demonstrating the new British Saxophone Quartet repertoire to (left) Nestor Koval, leader of the Pittsburgh Saxophone Quartet, and (centre) Raymond Beckenstein, leader of the New York Saxophone Quartet, and members of their quartets.

10 Woodwind Workshop

For ten consecutive years, 1973-82, Christopher Gradwell and the London Saxophone Quartet organized an annual School for Woodwind players known as the Woodwind Workshop. After an experimental non-residential course at the American School in London, where I was teaching at the time, we moved to Stockwell College, Bromley, and later to St Mary's College, Strawberry Hill, Twickenham.

We always agreed that the Woodwind Workshop was by far the most satisfying and enjoyable enterprise of all the LSQ's many and varied activities, but over the years it took an ever increasing toll of our energies and finances.

We never made any profit, and were usually lucky if we covered the cost of the many deputies we had to put into our various West End shows and regular teaching jobs. This was because we insisted on maintaining the highest possible standard for the evening concerts, engaging woodwind players of international stature, and we always paid our resident teachers and visiting lecturers rates commensurate with what they could earn elsewhere for recording sessions.

We all agreed that we would not wish to continue running the Woodwind Workshop if it were no longer financially viable to maintain those standards.

So, eventually, we had to wind it up, but we were left with ten years of very happy memories, and I'm still on the lookout for that eccentric millionaire woodwind fanatic who would like to start it all up again!

THE 1973 BRITISH WOODWIND WORKSHOP

The American School in London was the scene of the first ever British Woodwind Workshop. Although its success was the result of many people's efforts and the sponsorship of Henri Selmer, Paris, the main credit must undoubtedly to to Christopher Gradwelll. His was the idea in the first place, and his meticulous long-term planning and untiring co-ordination of activities were the principal factors in what proved to be an unprecedented exchange of woodwind music and ideas.

So much seems to have transpired over the four days that I can only mention a few of the highlights. Lecturers on the first day were Stephen Trier of the London Philharmonic, who discussed the orchestral development of the bass clarinet and saxophone, and Edward Planas, American born (but luckily for us, English resident) woodwind acoustician. In two brilliant lectures Ted explored the mystic regions of nodes and antinodes with a degree of clarity, erudition and wit seldom displayed in this esoteric field.

The first evening concert was given by the Zephyrus Woodwind Quintet; Edward Beckett (flute), Sara Barrington (oboe), John Stenhouse (clarinet), James Beck (horn) and Brian Wightman (bassoon).

For me, the most interesting work in the programme was Frank Cordell's *Interplay*; one of the finest new woodwind quintet works to have been written in this country for many years, and a brilliant example of what a really professional composer can do with this combination. The concert ended with Malcolm Arnold's *Sea Shanties*; one of the few pieces which make me bounce up and down in my seat with pure joy, like a fat little boy at a Christmas treat!

After another day of Master Classes on all the woodwind instruments, the second evening recital was given by 'Mr English Clarinet' himself, Jack Brymer. He gave the best performance of the Poulenc and Brahms E flat Sonatas I have ever heard, and between these major works presented a dazzling variety of styles, ranging from my favourite clarinet and piano work, Malcolm Arnold's Sonatina, to a new soprano saxophone piece by Colin Cowles. All were delivered with incomparable panache and inimitably relaxed introductions.

Next day there happened one of those happenings which make this drab old life seem worthwhile. James Houlik, noted tenor saxophone specialist of the University of East Carolina was passing through London on the way to record in Holland. He called me up to say 'Hi'. A fatal thing to do to an assistant deputy Woodwind Workshop co-ordinator in the full throes of co-ordinating. 'Come and give us a quick blast at the old Woodwind Workshop,' I said. Next thing I knew we were all agog at the most brilliant lecture-recital I've ever heard on any wind instrument. Jim talked and played so fluently and musically that he literally changed the lives of many present. One of the students has told me since that he has changed his career plans to become a tenor saxophone recitalist. I myself have laid aside innumerable commissions for clarinet duets (below the break) and racy articles on the breeding habits of gerbils, to write Jim a tenor saxophone concerto.

After the final day of Clarinet Choirs, Woodwind Choirs and a students concert, the final evening concert was upon us. It opened with the first performance of a saxophone quartet by Geoffrey Grey, played by the co-ordinator, deputy co-ordinator, assistant deputy co-ordinator and deputy assistant co-ordinator of the Woodwind Workshop, who are sometimes known collectively as the London Saxophone Quartet. They were then joined by Britain's leading trumpeter John Wilbraham, in a transcription of an Albinoni Concerto for piccolo, trumpet and saxophone quartet.

Next I played the first performance of a Concertino for soprano saxophone and Chamber Orchestra by the eccentric East Twickenham composer, Paul Harvey, which he has dedicated to Paul Brodie. (Not to me, the snob!) The orchestra was conducted by Christopher Gradwell ... look, I know this is all getting a bit incestuous, but we were having a good time, and it gets better after the interval.

It certainly did; I've been saving this guy up till last for the big fanfare ... Woodwind Workshop's resident professor of saxophone ... all the way from Crodell, Oklahoma ... up and coming All-American saxophone virtuoso Robert Black. Accompanied by his charming and talented new wife, Patricia ... (Hold it right there, folks, for a word from our sponsor ... Why not spend YOUR honeymoon next year at Ye Olde Brittishe Woodwinde Workshoppe? Happy newly-weds Bobby and Patti Black said, 'We were so bored with Niagara Falls and the Grand Canyon, we decided to make the British woodwind scene, and enjoyed every minute with these quaint, charming people. We even heard real live 'flautists playing their flauts, and 'clarinettists' in 'programmes' of 'Colourful' clarinet music!' The 1974 Y.O.B.W.W. will be held the last week in August at Stockwell College, Bromley, Kent (The Garden of England), within easy reach of the fleshpots and reed shops of swinging London. Where was I? ... oh, yes ... Mr Black played alto saxophone and piano works by Charles Koechlin and Karel Husa, and then brought the Workshop to a brilliant conclusion with the Gradwell Chamber Orchestra in Ibert's *Concertino da Camera*.

Look, I'm worried at the way this serious article has degenerated into cheap humour... (sorry, 'Humor'... I'm going all to pieces!) I can't finish it in the standard required by Woodwind World. There's this cat I see in the pub... Bill something... long hair and beard ... achieved some success with plays in blank verse ... for the price of a pint he's adapted one of his bits to sum the whole thing up... Henry V, act IV, scene II, I think he called it... anyway, over to you, Bill...

> This day is called the feast of Woodwind:
> He that outlives this day, and comes safe home,
> Will stand a tip-toe when this day is nam'd,
> And rouse him at the name of Woodwind.
> He that shall live this day, and see old age,
> Will yearly on the vigil feast his neighbours,
> And say, 'Tomorrow is Woodwind Workshop:'
> Then will he pull his lip and show his scars;
> And say, 'These wounds I had on Woodwind's day.'
> Old men forget: yet all shall be forgot,
> But he'll remember with advantages
> What feats he did that day. Then shall our names,
> Familiar in his mouth as household words,
> Gradwell the king, Lawrence and Hambleton,
> Brymer and Harvey, Bobby Black and Houlik.
> Be in their flowing cups freshly remember'd.
> This story shall the REED-man teach his son;
> And Woodwind Workshop shall ne'er go by.
> From this day to the ending of the world,
> But we in it shall be remembered;
> We few, we happy few, we band of brothers;
> For he today that licks his reed with me
> Shall be my brother; be he ne'er so vile
> This day shall gentle his condition:
> Saxophonists in England now a-bed
> Shall think themselves accurs'd they were not here,
> And hold their manhoods cheap whiles any speaks
> That play'd with us 'pon Woodwind Workshop day.

What is a Woodwind Workshop? It's possible that the term might conjure up in some people's minds a room full of benches at which elderly brown-overalled craftsmen minister gently to the wasted keywork of ailing hecklephones and the congested tone-holes of neglected contra-bassoons. This image, appealing though it may be, is inaccurate. Here, the application of the word 'Workshop' is more akin to that term so beloved by American music educators, 'Clinic'. (That conjures up the same image as 'Workshop', but the craftsmen wear white overalls and rimless glasses). I suppose 'Workshop' in this context might be defined as, 'people doing and talking about something they're good at, to other people who would like to become better at it'.

This is a fair general description of the Woodwind Workshop. It all started last August, at the American School in St. John's Wood, London. At least, that was the four day culmination of months of planning, co-ordinated by one of the few woodwind players in this country who could have coped with such an undertaking, Christopher Gradwell. He is basically a clarinet player, having studied that instrument under John Davies at the Royal Academy of Music. He had always been interested in the saxophone, but had studied it more seriously than most clarinettists who double. On leaving the Academy, Christopher decided to use his saxophone prowess to broaden his knowledge of the music profession and to see the world at the same time. He joined the band on the Queen Mary, and plied back and forth across the Atlantic, becoming a polished dance band player and jazz soloist, and learning a lot about different sorts of people and life in general. (Actually, that's the most interesting part, especially that time in Buenos Aires when . . . but that's not within the scope of this article . . . besides, he might sue me!)

Eventually, he decided it was time to heave his sea chest ashore and, saluting the quarterdeck for the last time, he stepped on to Southampton hard. His pockets jingling with Spanish gold (those gigs in Montevideo) he popped into a dockside tavern to wash the salt from his throat. When he emerged at closing time, the dreaded Press Gang was out. He remembers the hoarse shout of a burly Petty Officer, 'Ar, me'arties, there be a prime tenor player if ever I clapped eyes on 'un!' The characteristic gait of the seafaring saxophonist had betrayed our hero to his pursuers, and the next thing he knew, he was chained to four other reedmen in the pit of the infamous London Palladium, crashing into the overture of the Tomblebert Humperjones Spectacular. From this base he later emerged to play with LSO, Philharmonia and BBC Symphony Orchestra, but the main product of this period of his career was a series of original and enterprising ideas, the ramifications of which are well on the way to revolutionising the woodwind scene in this country.

The 1974 Woodwind Workshop got under way with three times as many enrolments as the previous year. For the first time it was a residential course, being held at Stockwell College of Education, Bromley. The organisers were, once again, the London Saxophone

Quartet, assisted by a distinguished panel of woodwind experts, consisting of: Jerome Bunke (clarinet) from New York, Norbert Nozy (saxophone) from Belgium, Christopher Taylor and Adrian Brett (flutes), Robin Miller (oboe), Brian Sewell and Anton Weinberg (bassoons), Barry Robinson (jazz saxophone) and Victor Slaymark (clarinet). Visiting lecturers were Ted Planas, who gave daily talks on the acoustics and design of all the woodwind family; Stephen Trier on the basset horn, bass and contrabass clarinets; Alan Hacker on early clarinets, and the distinguished composer Frank Cordell, on writing music for the Media.

An extensive exhibition, illustrating the development of woodwind instruments from 1800 ws prepared by the noted collector, Paul Sargent, and was on view in the cafeteria throughout the five days. On the other side of this room Joe Proctor, of the Bromley Music Centre, set up a fine display of music, instruments and accessories, which was a focal point of interest for everybody at the Workshop.

Each evening there was a concert, the first being a London Saxophone Quartet recital. This included the first performance of Carey Blyton's *Flying Birds* Variations; a concert version, prepared by the composer, of his music for a Royal Society for the Protection of Birds film of the same name.

The second day finished with an informal musical evening, at which several bizarre items were perpetrated, including a genealogical dissertation on the 'Oon' family, by Paul Sargent, a duet by Paul Harvey for sopranino and bass saxophones, entitled *Bubble and Squeak*, played by the composer and David Lawrence, and the same composer's gruesome epic of pastoral violence, *The Tale of the Three Billy Goats Gruff and the Troll*, for saxophone quartet and narrator.

Carey Blyton struck again at this concert; he came up to me in the bar just before it started, and thrust the parts of a new saxophone quartet piece into my clammy hands. 'When I got home after *Flying Birds* yesterday,' he said, 'I sat up all night writing this for your musical evening.' I stumbled onto the stage and stuck the parts in front of the lads, snarling, 'Play that . . . three, four . . .' and so *Mock Joplin* received its World Premiere!

On the third evening our distinguished overseas visitors shared a recital, both being accompanied by Martin Jones. In the first half Jerome Bunke gave dynamic performances of: Aria No 1 by Elliot Schwartz, the Martinu Sonatina, Meditazione by Karolyi Pal, the Bernstein Sonata and the Weber Concertino. After the interval Nobert Nozy gave a brilliant alto saxophone recital, consisting of a

Mule transcription of a Bach Sonata, Francois Daneels' Unaccompanied Suite, *Wheels Within Wheels* by Claude Coppens and Jean Absil's *Fantasie Caprice*.

The following evening it was the turn of the students, who produced a very varied programme, including items for clarinet choir, woodwind choir, flute quartet, saxophone quartet and the Mozart Sinfonia Concertante. Tony Spencer played an unaccompanied clarinet piece I had written for him to play in the Cousins Memorial Competition at Kneller Hall, and I'm delighted to report that he later won the first prize.

The final concert was a programme of woodwind concerti with string orchestra, conducted by Christopher Gradwell. The first soloist was Robin Miller, in the Cimarosa-Benjamin Oboe Concertino. Then Hale Hambleton gave the first performance of Eric Hughes' Concerto de Camera for Clarinet and Strings; one of the finest new clarinet works I have heard for a very long time. Christopher Taylor closed the first half with the Bach B minor Flute Suite. After the interval Joanna Graham principal bassoonist of the BBC Concert Orchestra, played the Gordon Jacob Bassoon Concerto, and I followed with the Villa-Lobos Fantasia for soprano saxophone, three horns and strings. The LSQ finished the concert with Pierre-Max Dubois' Concerto Grosso for saxophone quartet, strings and percussion, in which the orchestra was directed by Christopher Taylor.

So our second Woodwind Workshop came to an end; we had all learnt a great deal from one another, and, I hope, made some contribution towards the woodwind scene in Britain, by demonstrating anew the beauties and fascination of these wonderful instruments and their music.

Five B flat contrabass clarinets assembled at the Woodwind Workshop.

Christopher Gradwell conducting Soprano Concertino.

Paul Harvey rehearsing a clarinet trio consisting of: Caroline Hobbs and Karen Pickering (both aged 12) and Paulina Harvey (aged nine).

The Clarinet Choir, which rehearsed every afternoon during the Workshop.

I think it was Malcolm Arnold who said, 'When you pick up a conductor's baton, you can feel the POWER running up your arm!' Personally I only indulge if it's something I've written, or nobody else wants to do it! In this case, both conditions applied!

The third annual Woodwind Workshop was once again held at Stockwell College, Bromley. Many of the most popular features from previous years were repeated, such as Ted Planas' fascinating discourses on acoustics and instrument construction, but there were several new aspects. Most notable was the inclusion of the horn, which of course made a much wider variety of repertoire possible under the guidance of Neill Sanders. New members of this year's faculty were Brian Sewell (bassoon), John McCaw (clarinet) and, from the Bordeaux Conservatoire, Jean-Marie Londeix (saxophone).

On the first evening the distinguished film producer, James Archibald showed his film 'Music' which he made for the British Music Council. It depicts the wide variety of musical events which take place in the course of one day. The organisers of the Workshop, the London Saxophone Quartet, entertained on the following evening, with a concert of an unusual format. Our guest in the first half was the soprano. Susan Roe, who was accompanied by various members of the LSQ in Gordon Jacob's Songs with clarinet, Stravinsky's 'Elegy for JFK' and 'Berceuses du Chat', finally all together in Paul Harvey's new work for soprano and saxophone quartet, 'The Seven Deadly Virtues'. In the second half, Barry Robinson, who takes the jazz saxophone classes, took over the LSQ as his sax section in a selection of numbers such as Kenton's 'Opus in Pastel' and some BBC Radio Orchestra features for sax section.

The third evening recital was shared by Christopher Taylor (flute) Robin Miller (oboe) and Brian Sewell (bassoon), accompanied by Martin Jones. They played various solo items and the Poulenc trio, Christopher Taylor rounding off the evening with a formidable rendering on the piccolo of variations on 'The Carnival of Venice'.

The Thursday recital was again a shared one, this time by Jean-Marie Londeix and John McCaw, each being accompanied by Martin Jones. On Friday it was the turn of the members of the course, who produced a very varied programme of an extremely high standard.

The final concert consisted of large wind works, conducted by Christopher Gradwell. The Gounod 'Petit Symphony', the Strauss Serenade and the Mozart Thirteen Wind made a fitting conclusion to another very successful week of woodwind study and enjoyment.

11 The London Saxophone Quartet

It is now three years since the LSQ 'retired from public life', and perhaps this is as good a time as any to review its sixteen years existence with objective hindsight and to assess its achievements.

The situation in 1969 was this: I had recently returned to London from the Bournemouth Symphony Orchestra, had just started teaching at Kneller Hall, and was playing the musical version of *Anne of Green Gables* at the New Theatre (now the Albery) in St Martin's Lane. The only saxophone quartet in the country up till then had been the Michael Krein Quartet, which used to do mainly light music broadcasts, such as a series called *Music in Miniature*. Michael Krein had recently died, however, but Chester Smith, the alto player, had taken over the running of the quartet and kept the library. He had persuaded Jack Brymer to take over the leadership of the quartet, even to the extent of using Micky Krein's old soprano. Gordon Lewin and Norman Barker were the other two most regular members.

About this time Terry Busby started a group called 'The London Clarinet Sextet', in which I played contrabass. Here I met Christopher Gradwell, and he engaged me to play alto saxophone in a performance of Walton's *Facade* which he was conducting at a concert in the Conway Hall, Red Lion Square (scene of many a stormy Musicians' Union meeting). David Lawrence was playing clarinet and bass clarinet in *Facade*, and Chris had the idea of recruiting another saxophone player and including some quartets in the programme. So our first public quartet performance had me on soprano, Chris on alto, Geoff Williams on tenor and Dave on baritone.

I think we played the Mule arrangement of the three Albeniz pieces; people seemed to like the sound, and we thought about doing it again. However, Geoff went off to do a season in Bermuda and I went off to Switzerland with the London Symphony

Orchestra. I was playing tenor saxophone in Prokofiev's *Romeo and Juliet* and Hale Hambleton was playing bass clarinet. I have a mental picture of us both sitting on music baskets backstage in the Zurich Tonhalle, Hale tenderly massaging the tip of a bass clarinet reed with fine emery paper as I extolled the wholesome delights of saxophone quartet playing.

When we returned to London, Hale joined us on alto, Chris moved on to tenor, and we were in business. Our first concerts were prodigiously serious affairs. Encased in immaculate tails, we battered the audience (and our chops) into submission with uncut performances of the major works of the saxophone quartet repertoire; Pierné, Schmitt and Glazounov (yes, even the dreaded 'Schumann Variation', known in the trade as the 'Cheap Trill). Gradually we evolved the much more varied programme which became the LSQ hallmark; a strong opening piece which demonstrated the range and dynamics of the saxophone quartet. Then a set of early music transcriptions; this was always my favourite field for quartet arranging, as most medieval and renaissance music was intended to be played on shawms, crumhorns, cornetts, serpents, recorders; whatever was available at the time, so saxophones are equally viable. We usually finished the first half with the most substantial work of the evening; one of the Jacob quartets, for instance, or a French work.

The second half generally started with a set of light/classical transcriptions in Krein Quartet style; indeed, we eventually bought the Krein library. Then we would veer more to the jazz side, in pieces we mainly had especially written for us, the most successful being those by Neil Richardson.

The concert would finish with something of a rabble-rousing nature, often my *Robert Burns Suite*. Just looking at a set of Scottish bagpipes, it always seemed to me obvious that the chanter and three drones were crying out to be mimicked by a saxophone quartet. There were times in the following decade and a half when I wished I'd never thought of it, but that's the way the bannock breaks!

In our first few concerts we just sat and played, in dignified string quartet fashion. However, came one concert when the programme was all printed in the wrong order, so I had to stand up between each piece to tell the audience what we were going to play next. There were several other amusing misprints in the programme as well as the order, and I couldn't resist the odd jocular comment on these. We couldn't help noticing how much warmer and more receptive the audience became, having had a mild chuckle between the items, to relieve the concentration of listening. 'Chat' was in forever after that, and we always assigned our respective chatting spots to each other before each concert. Everybody does it now, of course, but then it was quite a new idea!

Our only change of personnel, apart from Anton Weinberg depping for Hale on the Spain/Greece tour, was in 1978, when it became increasingly difficult for Hale to fit in the LSQ engagements with his permanent job as co-principal clarinet of English National Opera, so he asked us to phase him out gradually and let someone else take over the alto chair.

Peter Ripper, at that time a member of the BBC Radio Orchestra, had depped for Hale on a number of occasions, and was the obvious choice. Peter joined us for the Middle East tour, the Tenth Anniversary concert at St John's, Smith Square, and was a stalwart member of the LSQ for its remaining seven years.

The main reasons for the LSQ's retirement in 1985 were, as usual, economic. Income from LSQ engagements had never been a large percentage of our personal incomes, and much of it was ploughed back into the quartet fund for administration expenses, commissioning new works, buying new music, etc. Dave Lawrence once described the LSQ as 'the most exlusive and expensive club in London'.

One problem was that the Inland Revenue seemed to have confused the abbreviation 'LSQ' with, possibly, ICI, EMI or IBM, and was continually sending us bills more communsurate with enterprises of that financial stature!

We were all doing shows and teaching in order to earn an honest crust, and it became less and less viable to leave town for a whole day and most of the following night just to do one concert for a provincial music society. They could not afford to pay the sort of fee which would cover our deputies for a day's teaching and a show for all four of us. Then Chris started his 'Versatile Music' orchestra contracting business, and no longer had time or organize the LSQ, so at that point we rode away into the sunset.

Looking back over the sixteen years, my main recollections are the good times and laughs with the boys, especially on the foreign tours, some of which are chronicled elsewhere in this book. Taking the broad view of our achievements, it is certainly true that the LSQ put the saxophone quartet on the musical map; as there are now quite a few very good quartets carrying on the work. Even more important, the saxophone is now being taught officially at all the principal schools of music, which was certainly not the case twenty years ago.

But I feel that the LSQ's main achievement can best be appreciated by glancing through a reference book by an American author, James Dawson. It's called *Music for Saxophone by British Composers*. When he told me he was compiling this, I remember being rather sceptical as to the amount of music he would find. However, I was amazed on seeing the finished bibliography, especially at the amount of saxophone quartet music written for the LSQ. Let this stand as our epitaph!

J'ACCUSE!
A biting indictment of the BBC by the leader of an oppressed minority group

YEVRAH LUAP, the author of this article, is founder of 'Daleks' Lib', and is a keen jazz historian. His book 'Venusian Jazz' will be well-known to many Crescendo *readers. Last year he was elected an honorary fellow of the Martian Academy of Electronic Music.*

A blatant contravention of the Race Relations Act will take place on Britain's TV screens on the four Saturdays following February 23. That camp Time Lord, Dr Who, will be undertaking another of his epic adventures, entitled 'Death To The Daleks'.

As if this inflammatory title, equating us in the public's mind with 'Baddy' minority groups such as Red Indians and Nazis, were not insult enough to the law-abiding Dalek community of Great Britain, an even more sinister trend has been brought to my attention.

As all musicians know, the success of the Dr Who series has been mainly due to the inspired background music and effects created by a small group of talented Dalek composers and technicians working at the BBC Radiophonic Workshop. They are doubtless a familiar sight to many of you who work at Maida Vale Studios, as they glide into the canteen at lunchtime to purchase their humble repast of sausage and chips, yoghurt and a pint of oil.

Yet, though our people were brought from the home planet by the BBC to create this great TV series, they are now being cast aside like burnt-out transistors. For the BBC now stands revealed in its true human chauvinist colours. A human composer has

151

written the music for these episodes. What is more, a composer well-known for his reactionary humanistic tendencies; the notorious Carey Blyton, president of the militant Swanley branch of the 'Earth For Humans' society.

As if this were not bad enough, an even worse insult has come to light through the photographic evidence of an intrepid Dalek investigator who penetrated the inner recesses of the BBC Lime Grove Studios last week, disguised as a moog synthesiser. His dramatic photograph, taken by means of a special telephoto attachment now fitted to the Dalek Mark VI, shows human musicians engaged in the recording of Blyton's score.

At least, upon close inspection, they appear to be more or less human; they are certainly not Daleks, anyway. Informed sources believe them to be a group known as The London Saxophone Quartet. As if there were not enough Dalek saxophone players in the MU to undertake these sessions! But all this is just the tip of the iceberg! When viewed in conjunction with the genocidal title 'Death To The Daleks', who can blame us if we charge up our exterminator batteries and close up our ranks to await the inevitable confrontation with the human race?

IMPORTANT COMMERCIAL RECOGNITION FOR THE SAXOPHONE QUARTET

One of the institutions of British television is the children's science fiction series *Dr Who*, which is now in its tenth year. The BBC commissions various leading composers to write the incidental music, and recently asked Carey Blyton, who is Professor of Composition for Films and Television at Guildhall School of Music, to score a four-part series entitled *Death to the Daleks*. (Daleks are highly intelligent beings who inhabit robot-like bodies, bristling with armaments and gadgets, which they manipulate by psychokinetic impulses). I'm glad you asked me that!

Mr Blyton, who has already written several works for the London Saxophone Quartet, including the incidental music for two documentary films, decided to score the entire series for saxophone quartet and one percussion player. The London Saxophone Quartet: Paul Harvey, Hale Hambleton, Christopher Gradwell and David Lawrence, with Ronald Macrea (percussion) spent two days at BBC Lime Grove Stuidos recording the score under Carey Blyton's direction.

It is vivid, dramatic, and at times horrible music, including some most effective organum plainchant, to which an electronically multiplied human voice was added to represent the Exxilon's human sacrificial rituals.

The series is now being transmitted weekly, with the LSQ credited with the playing of the music on the end titles of each episode. This is the point which is so important for the cause of the saxophone, as millions of people who would never dream of attending a concert or even listening to a serious music program on sound radio, will perhaps be given some idea of the saxophone's possibilities. When other musicians and composers hear music of the high quality of Carey Blyton's writings for saxophone quartet, it can only be good for the development of saxophone, in whatever field of music it may be heard.

THE LITTLE BIG BAND
AN EXPERIMENT IN BRASS AND WOODWIND FRATERNISATION

The London Gabrieli Brass and the London Saxophone Quartet are two chamber groups with much in common, despite their different instrumentation. Both are basically classical (straight, serious, call it what you will) groups who have come to realize, after playing many concerts all over Britain and abroad, that it is vital to present audiences with as wide a variety of musical styles as possible. To this end both groups have commissioned many new works, transcriptions of old music and jazz arrangements.

The Gabrieli and the LSQ first played together on an album for Charisma Records of poetry by the Poet Laureate, Sir John Betjeman. All the music was written by Jim Parker, an oboist and pianist who has been making an increasingly big name for himself over the last few years with his Television music and as Musical Director of the versatile music-poetry group, the Barrow Poets. The album, entitled *Betjeman's Banana Blush*, proved so popular that another, *Late Flowering Love*, soon followed with more or less the same personnel.

When this was finished, everyone agreed they had so enjoyed playing Jim Parker's music, that an attempt should be made to interest a record company in making an album of music alone. Christopher Gradwell, the manager of the LSQ, set to work on the project in his inimitable style, and eventually came up with a contract from Canon Records. Jim Parker also set to work, and very quickly came up with fourteen numbers, some originals, some highly individual arrangements of standards such as *The Umbrella Man*. At last the great day arrived, and EMI Abbey Road Studios was the genesis of The Little Big Band. The personnel are as follows:

The London Gabrieli Brass: James Watson and Crispian Steele-Perkins (trumpets), Christopher Larkin (horn), Roger Groves (trombone), John Smith (tuba).

The London Saxophone Quartet: Paul Harvey (soprano saxophone, B flat clarinet and E flat clarinet), Hale Hambleton (alto saxophone, B flat and E flat clarinet), Christopher Gradwell (tenor saxophone, B flat and bass clarinet and flute), David Lawrence (baritone and bass saxophones, B flat and bass clarinet) plus a rhythm section of drums, bass and guitar-banjo.

We were so excited by the whole project that we invited Gerald Style, who is becoming known as 'The Musicians' Photographer', to roam the studio at will, so that a permanent pictorial record would exist of this unusual merging of two instrumental families.

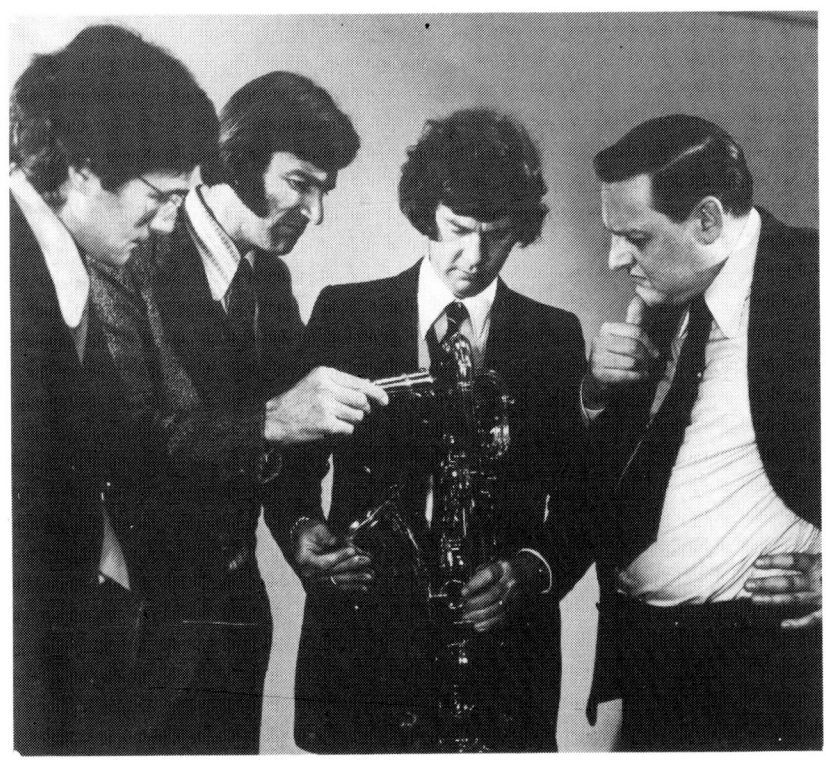

A knotty problem!

'The Little Big Band'.

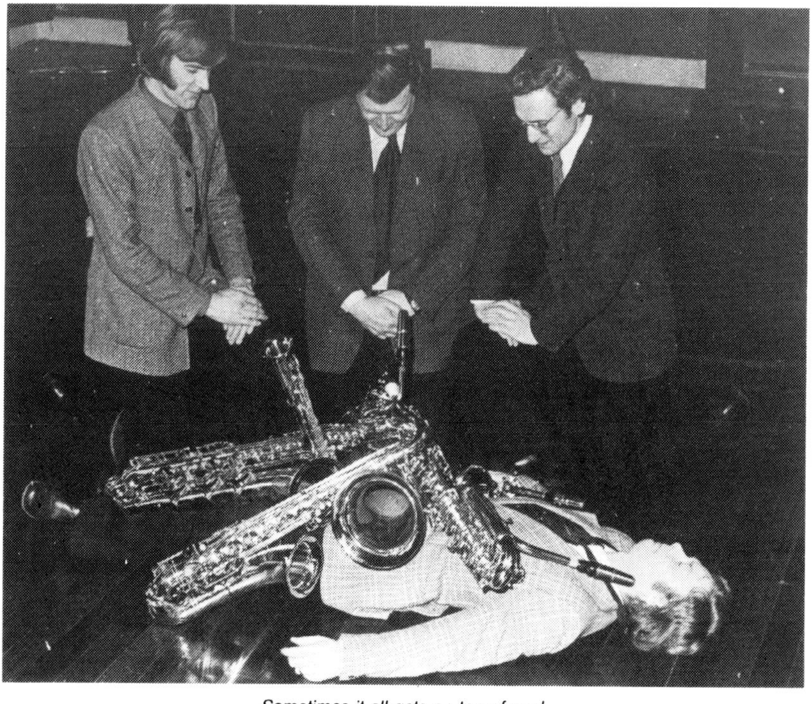

Sometimes it all gets on top of you!

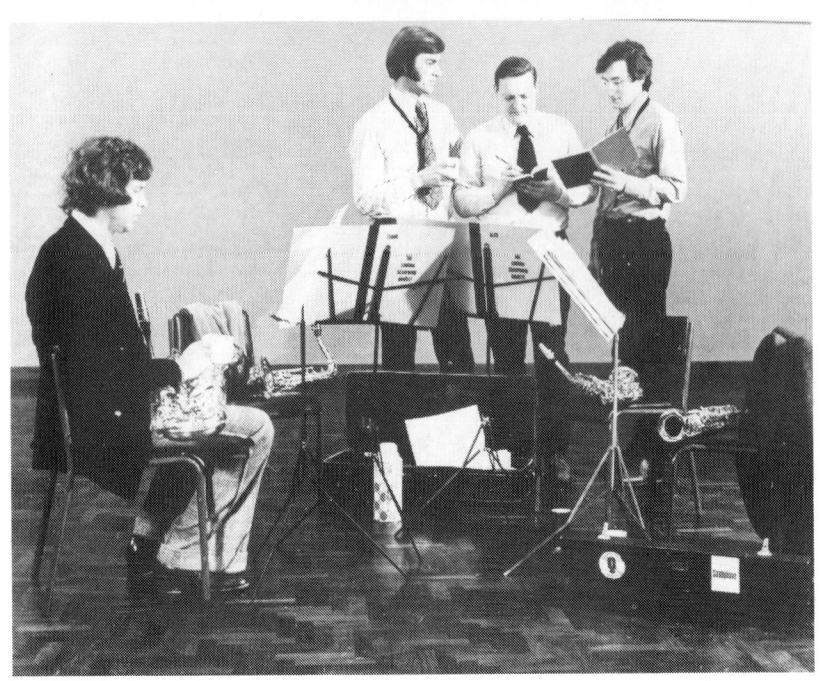

Someone isn't using . . .

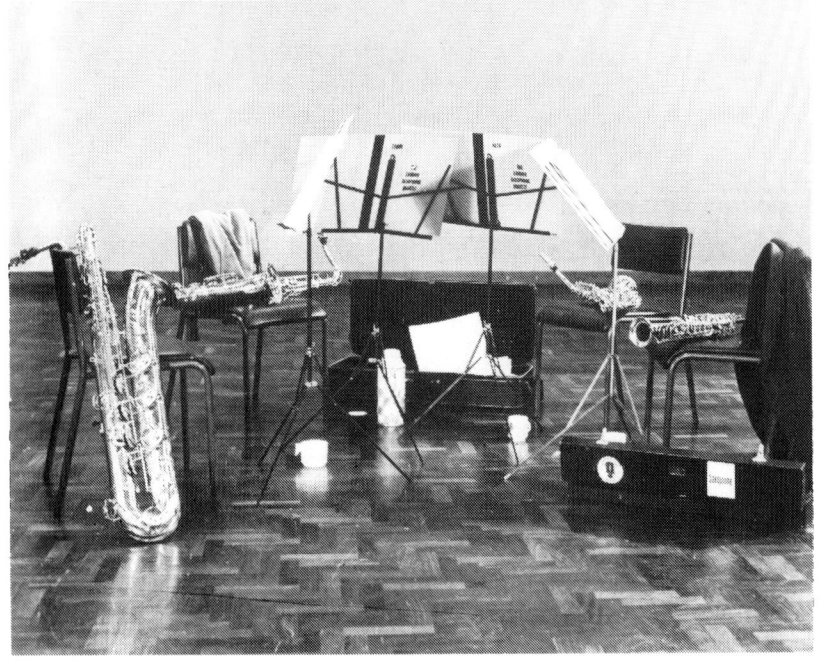

They're open!

The London Saxophone Quartet.

PUBLISH AND BE BANNED!

Wally Horwood, eminence grise of the controversial Egon Publishing conglomerate today spoke out to reporters from his mid-Thames tax haven, Eel Pie Island, which he shares with Paul Harvey, whose memoirs, *Reedbasher*, have been banned in Britain. Harvey, established Civil Servant, senior Professor of Music of the Ministry of Defence and, consequently, signatory to the Official Secrets Act, revealed details of top secret Army saxophone fingerings and other classified material in his book, previously entitled *Bandroom Jottings*.

Horwood's proud boast is that, no matter how dull and uncontroversial an author's subject may be, Egon Publishers will guarantee to get his book banned in Britain and involved in a number of interminable court cases. Their most notable successes in the musical field so far have been *Lady Chatterley's Bassoon Teacher*, *The Last Temptation Of Herbert Von Karajan* and *I Was A Teenage Werewolf For The Arts Council Of Great Britain*.

I had been following the Spycatcher *saga with great interest and envy,* said Horwood, *and was racking my brains for a musical equivalent. Then I met Harvey, who said he had been trying for years to get his tutor,* The Complete Clarinet Player, *banned, but unfortunately the government didn't seem to object to it. So we put our heads together and came up with this* Reedbasher *idea.*

Harvey, 53-year-old, pear-shaped expatriate Yorkshireman, took up the story. *For years I've been churning out clarinet and saxophone music, tutors, exercises and technical articles, and never a single injunction, libel suit or even a few controversial reviews! It's all so discouraging; I decided it was high time to zap up my image or go back to intensive tortoise breeding!*

Mrs M. Thatcher, well-known Prime Minister, said, *Ever since the* Spycatcher *business it's been a problem getting out of the end of Downing Street for the crowds of publishers hanging around in Whitehall hoping to pick up civil servants' memoirs. The only solution is to ban so many new publications that they no longer receive any publicity. Anyway, that Harvey person is much too keen on side key B flat and the chromatic F sharp key for my liking. I always use the* Otto Langey Tutor *myself!*

Officers of the Special Branch sat sipping pints of beer very slowly outside the picturesque Twickenham riverside pub, *The Barmy Arms*, watching Eel Pie Island in case Harvey or Horwood tried to slip back to the mainland. Meanwhile, teams of lawyers came and went across the narrow bridge, negotiating such deals as flim rights and translation into Serbo-Croat.

From WINDS Magazine, Summer, 2188

The Authentic Performance of 20th Century Clarinet and Saxophone Music
by Holly Warhood

The recent discovery of the book *Bandroom Jottings*, dating from the late 20th century, throws much new light on the instruments and performance techniques of the period of which little has so far been known owing to the destruction of so many recordings and videos in the Martian War of Independence (2075–83).

The main difference in the instruments was that they were much lighter than ours, as they did not require lead shielding for the internal nuclear rods. The best clarinets were actually made of WOOD; incredible to think of nowadays; a clarinet with a completely wooden body sold for as little as £1,000 in the 1980s!

Now that elegant ladies of fashion display their wealth with wooden necklaces, earrings and bracelets, wood, produced by the long, difficult and expensive process of growing trees, being one of the most costly materials, while any schoolboy can manufacture unlimited gold and platinum with his home chemistry set, reproduction 20th century clarinets of pure wood are not a viable possibility for most players. The exception, of course, being the popular Venusian clarinettist, Ned Mahjonn, who's image as *The Man with the Wooden Clarinet* and quaint Venusian accent, seems to have caught the public's imagination.

For really authentic performances of 20th century music, however, a wooden reed is essential. Genuine 'Arundo Donax' bamboo cane is now being grown intensively in the State Horticultural Factory at Kew, and a reproduction 20th century reed can be purchased for a mere £50,000. With proper care this reed should last you at least three years and you will be able to delight discerning audiences with the squeaks and chirps which were such a distinctive feature of clarinet and saxophone playing in those gracious and elegant days.

Instrument makers of today must supply products suitable for the multi-racial interplanetary population; Earth's minority groups of Martian immigrants, Saturnian guest-workers and Plutonian Hopping Bands must be catered for. Two hundred years ago things were much simpler; the humanoid population of Earth was almost exclusively equipped with a standard two arms with fingers on each hand and one head with a single mouth. The same tutor and fingering chart would do for pupils all over the world!

Contrast this with the situation today, when a firm such as Music Sales exports twenty seven different versions of Harvey's *Complete Clarinet Player* to as many different planets! Incidentally, Boosey and Hawkes tell me that the Otto Langey Saxophone Tutor still sells well on Uranus, but the title of *Tune A Day* has had to be changed for some planets, where a day can last for up to ten earth years!

But I digress; you want to know what techniques will give your performance that authentic 20th century style. It was common practice to take breaths between phrases; circular breathing was known but only rarely used as a special effect. Tonguing was, for the most part, single, with only occasional bursts of double or triple; again, you must bear in mind that the vast majority of players had only one tongue, and of the non-forked variety, at that.

None of the keys were power-assisted, even on baritone saxophones, so you must limit the speed of your trills to your fingers' capability. Multiphonics and saxophone altissimo register notes were not produced electronically but by a knowledge of the harmonic series and a combination of diaphragm, air column, throat, oral cavity, embouchure and fingering; a series of physical disciplines which would amply repay study by the student of today.

Authenticity in performance of early music is likely to become a sought after commodity in the Arts Market Place of the future. Last year, archaeologists digging in the City of London uncovered the legendary underground Barbican Hall, and the concerts since given there in 20th century dress (tails 'n' long black), proved the most popular events of the 2187 season.

Holly Warhood is the author of the definitive biography
of the inventor of the Mercurian bagpipes:
AXEL DAPHOS 2014-2094 — *His Life and Legacy.*
(Egon Publishers Ltd., Lunar Industrial Estate, Earth Moon).

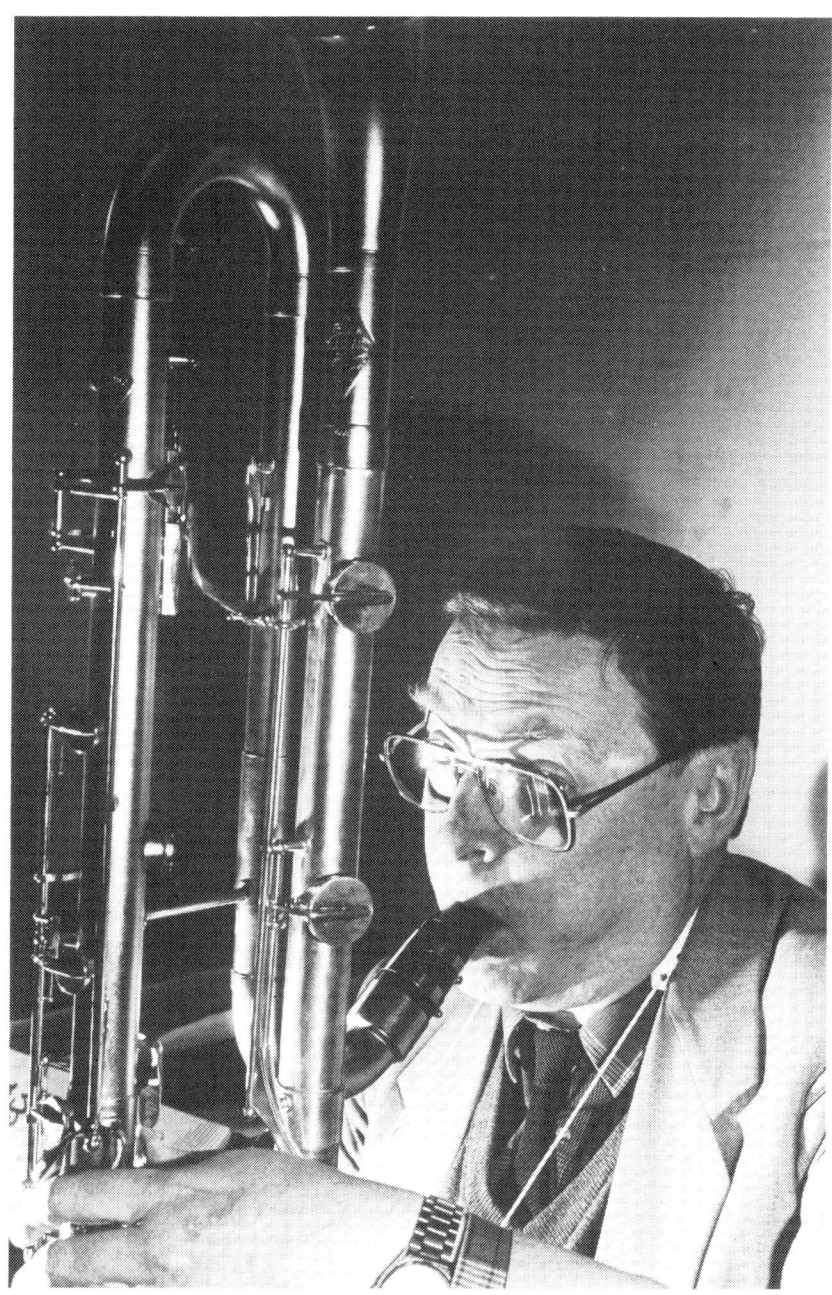
Paul Harvey with his BB flat Leblanc contrabass clarinet Bottom C extension by Peter Snowdon. (Photograph: Michael Farnham, Professor of Clarinet, Royal Military School of Music, Kneller Hall).

PAUL HARVEY — Publications for Clarinet

Title	Publisher
GRADED STUDY — DUETS for Two Clarinets (Two Volumes) FANTASIA IN ONE MOVEMENT for Four Clarinets	BOOSEY & HAWKES 295 Regent Street, London W1
SATIRICAL SUITE for Two Clarinets FOUR EASY TRIOS for Three Clarinets QUARTET for Three Clarinets and Bass Clarinet (Recorded by the Netherlands Clarinet Quartet on RCS 468)	SCHOTTS 48 Gt. Marlborough Street, London W1
IMPROVISATION ON A MARTIAL INVERSION for Unaccompanied Clarinet (Recorded by Paul Drushler on MRS 32641)	SHALLUMO PUBLICATIONS P.O. Box 2824, Rochester, NY 14626 USA
CONCERTO for Clarinet and Orchestra (Piano reduction) QUARTET for E flat Clarinet, B flat Clarinet, Basset Horn (or Alto Clarinet) and Bass Clarinet	EDITIONS MAURER 7 Avenue du Verseau, Brussels, Belgium
ALL AT SEA for Oboe and Clarinet	NEW WIND MUSIC 11 Park Chase, Wembley Park, Middlesex
CLARINET A LA CARTE, a Suite for Unaccompanied Clarinet PETS, a Suite for Unaccompanied Clarinet TEN TUNES FOR KATHY, a Suite for Unaccompanied Clarinet	RICORDI The Bury, Church Street, Chesham, Bucks
THE CLARINETTIST'S BEDSIDE BOOK USA Agents: Theodore Presser Co, Presser Place, Bryn Mawr, Pennsylvania, 19010 TEN FOR TWO Easy Duets for Flute and Clarinet or Two Clarinets	FENTONE MUSIC Earlstrees, Corby NN17 2SN
SONATA FOR CLARINET AND PIANO	SOUTHERN MUSIC CO., P.O. Box 329, San Antonio, Texas 78292 USA

Title	Publisher
TRIO for Flute (Alto), CLARINET and SAXOPHONE (Alto)	DORN PUBLICATIONS P.O. Box 206, 5 West Mill Street, Medfield, Massachusetts, 02052 USA
THREE ETUDES ON THEMES OF GERSHWIN for Unaccompanied Clarinet (Recorded by Gervase De Peyer on Chandos ABRD 1237 and by James Gillespie on MRS 32641)	CHAPPELL
THE COMPLETE CLARINET PLAYER (Four Volumes) DUETS AND STUDIES (Four Volumes)	MUSIC SALES 8/9 Frith Street, London, W1V 5TZ
'THE JAZZY CLARINET' Series for Clarinet and Piano	UNIVERSAL EDITION Kalmus Ltd., 38 Eldon Way, Paddock Wood, Tonbridge, Kent
VARIATIONS ON 'BONNY ENGLISH ROSE' for Clarinet and Piano CONTEST SOLOS a series for various instruments with Piano Accompaniment	STUDIO MUSIC CO. 77 Dudden Hill Lane, London NW10

These publications are also available from:
JUNE EMERSON WIND MUSIC, AMPLEFORTH, YORKS, ENGLAND

PAUL HARVEY — Publications for Saxophone

Title	Publisher
SEVEN SAXOPHONIAN FOLK DANCES for Saxophone Quartet British Agents: Fentone	KJOS MUSIC 4382 Jutland Drive, San Diego, California, 92117 USA
THE AGINCOURT SONG for Saxophone Quartet (Recorded by the LSQ on Transatlantic TRA 308) and RONCORP EMS 020 ROBERT BURNS SUITE for Saxophone Quartet (Recorded by the Paul Brodie Quartet on Golden Crest CRSQ 4154 and by The Fairer Sax on Saydisc CD-SLD 3 THE HARFLEUR SONG for Saxophone Quartet (Recorded by the LSQ on Argo 2K 79) CELTIC COLLAGE for Saxophone Quartet (Recorded by the LSQ on Argo 2K 79)	NOVELLOS Borough Green, Sevenoaks, Kent
CONCERTINO for SOPRANO Saxophone and Chamber Orchestra or Band (Piano reduction) (Recorded by Francois Daneels and the Belgian Radio Orchestra on Schott Freres Z 23) CONCERTINO for ALTO Saxophone and String Orchestra or Band (Piano reduction) CONCERTINO for TENOR Saxophone and Chamber Orchestra or Band (Piano reduction) CONCERTINO for BARITONE Saxophone and Chamber Orchestra or Band (Piano reduction)	EDITIONS MAURER 7 Avenue du Verseau, Brussels, Belgium
ALTO SAXOPHONE SOLOS with Piano Accompaniment (Two Volumes) TENOR SAXOPHONE SOLOS with Piano Accompaniment (Two Volumes) SAXOPHONE QUARTET ALBUMS Vol 1: Renaissance Dances and Madrigals Vol 2: Elizabethan and Baroque Keyboard Music	CHESTER MUSIC Eagle Court, London EC1

Title	Publisher
THE SAXOPHONIST'S BEDSIDE BOOK USA Agents: Theodore Presser Co., Presser Place, Bryn Mawr, Pennsylvania, 19010	FENTONE Fleming Road, Earlstrees, Corby, Northants
CONCERT DUETS for Alto and Tenor Saxophones BOLOGNA VARIATIONS by ROSSINI, arr. for Alto Saxophone and Piano SPANISH SERENADE by BIZET arr. for Alto or Soprano and Piano	RONCORP Inc. P.O. Box 724, Cherry Hill, New Jersey 08003, USA
SUITE from 'ACIS AND GALATEA' by HANDEL arr. for Saxophone Quartet SIX DUETS after Frederick Berr, and FIVE MORE DUETS for Alto and Tenor Saxophones	STUDIO MUSIC CO. 77 Dudden Hill Lane, London NW10
CONTEST SOLOS a series for various instruments with Piano Accompaniment (including Alto and Tenor Saxophones)	STUDIO MUSIC CO.
'EQUAL PARTNERS' PROGRESSIVE DUETS for Alto and Tenor Saxophones	CASCADE MUSIC 30 College Green, Bristol
SAXOPHONE SPECTRUM a series of flexibly scored Saxophone Ensembles	R. SMITH & CO. P.O. Box 367, Aylesbury, Bucks HP22 4LJ
'THE SINGING SAXOPHONE' a series of graded pieces for Alto or Tenor and Piano	STUDIO MUSIC CO.

These publications are also available from:
JUNE EMERSON WIND MUSIC, AMPLEFORTH, YORKS, ENGLAND